An Illustrated Dictionary of Cyborg Anthropology

By Amber Case

Illustrated by Maggie Wauklyn

Foreword by Douglas Rushkoff

For Sheldon

An Illustrated Dictionary of Cyborg Anthropology

Copyright © 2013 by Amber Case

Illustrations © 2013 by Maggie Wauklyn

Design and layout by Aaron Parecki

All rights reserved. No part of this book may be reproduced in any form by any electronic or mechanical means including photocopying, recording, or information storage and retrieval without permission in writing from the author.

Educators are free to copy and distribute this work for instructional purposes under the following conditions: You must attribute the text of this book to Amber Case, and attribute the illustrations to Maggie Wauklyn, you may not use this work for commercial purposes, and you may not alter or transform this work. For any other uses please contact Amber Case at case@cyborganthropology.com

ISBN-13: 978-1494773519
ISBN-10: 1494773511

www.cyborganthropology.com

Give feedback on the book at:
feedback@cyborganthropology.com

Third Edition
October 2014

Table of Contents

Foreword 7
Introduction 9
Cyborg 11
Affective Computing 15
Ambient Awareness 17
Anomie 19
Architecture Fiction 21
Asynchronous Communication 23
Celebrity as Cyborg 25
City as Software 27
Companion Species 29
Connective Obligation 31
Cyborg Security 33
Digital Backyard 35
Digital Hoarding 37
Diminished Reality 39
Equipotential Space 41
Extended Nervous System 43
Flow 45
Hertzian Space 47

Hyperlinked Memories 49
Identity Production 51
Interstitial Space 53
Invisible Space 55
Junk Sleep 57
Machine Learning 59
Mental Real Estate 61
Micro-singularity 63
Mundane Studies 65
Natural Language Processing . 67
Panic Architecture 69
Paracosmic Immersion 71
Path Dependence 73
Persistent Architecture 75
Prosthetics 77
Proxemics 79
Quantified Self 81
Robot 83
Secondhand Cyborg 85
Sighborg 87

Steve Mann 89
Synesthesia 91
Additional Reading 94
About the Author 98
About the Illustrator 99
Notes 100

Foreword

When I finally met Amber Case — whose writing and experiments I had been following for several years — I felt as if I had at last come in contact with the next iteration of human being. I have been writing about "screenagers" and "digital natives" since the early 90's, and interacting with one form or another of cyberpunk, hacker, or programmer since before even that.

But coming face to face with Case one rainy night in Portland, on the stairs to a bar no less, was like meeting the future I had always envisioned. We immediately found a step to share, and spent a half hour exchanging notes at breakneck speed. She jotted down ideas and phrases into her iPhone while I jotted them down with a pen on the little pad I carry around (of course we took a moment to compare form factors and usage patterns).

We ended up spending the majority of our antenna-touching simply exchanging our glossaries. "This is my term for when such and such happens," and "this is the way I express the feeling when…" Sure, we shared many of the same insights and experiences, but we seemed most concerned with arriving at a terminology — as if being able to name what was happening to us would help us cope with it better. At the very least, having a word or phrase we agreed on somehow ensured that we were describing the same phenomenon. That we were on the same page or, in more cyborg parlance, in sync.

Of course, Case is a generation or maybe two generations younger and more advanced than me at this point (younger generations being the latest model of human being, after all), and so her facility with and immersion in the cyborg society is more advanced than my own. I may have seen this all coming, but Case is the coming, itself. And unlike most of her peers — brilliant though they may be — Case doesn't simply muse on possibilities for a digitally engaged, gamified, and interactive society; she actually tests her hypotheses in the real world by launching everything from big games to research studies.

That's why when Case comes out with an entire book (as well as a living, growing web project) on the ever-expanding lexicon of the cyborg, we had all best take notice. For herein lies an effort to identify, codify, and articulate how what it means to be a human being is changing in a digital age. By developing a language for the era of cyborgs, Case is not just reporting on the digital frontier, but contextualizing and creating it. Just as God created the world with a word (read the beginning of the Bible for that part), Case — and the greater Cyborg Anthropology community — are building reality in real time.

My only real concern here is that readers not mistake the emerging reality depicted here for a dehumanized, pre-programmed, robotic landscape. Humans may soon become more intimate with machines and programs, but this doesn't mean we become more machine-like, ourselves. If we can manage to disconnect the future of technology from the industrial-age massification of labor and production that we just went through for the past five hundred years, we become capable of envisioning an implementation of technology that enhances the human, heightens the senses, and magnifies our agency. Just as eyeglasses help a person to see, our technologies can forge entirely human-to-human connections, enable mind-to-mind intimacy, and promote collaborative activities on a scale unimaginable to our pre-digital forebears.

So even if cut-and-paste becomes an approach to sexuality and genetics instead of just documents, this doesn't mean we will necessarily corrupt the code of human spirit beyond all recognition. We are, indeed, moving into an era when our tools will more than match the limits of our intentions. With nano, robotics, genomics, and programming, we do more than simply make stuff; we make stuff that goes on to make more stuff. We create robots and programs and entities that then go make new versions of themselves.

The intentions we embed into these technologies will live on. These are things not made or manufactured, but birthed and launched. They become partners that coexist with us on the cyborg landscape, and through their very presence they highlight for us what makes us uniquely human - and them not.

In order to navigate this new terrain of our own making, we deserve a language for describing and conceiving it. Call me old fashioned, but without the words, we have no idea what we are doing.

Douglas Rushkoff, Oct. 2011

Introduction

The idea that we are all cyborgs is not new. As Donna Haraway was quoted in 1997, "the realities of modern life happen to include a relationship between people and technology so intimate that it's no longer possible to tell where we end and machines begin."[1]

Technology is so embodied in our everyday lives that it is often difficult to step back and realize how we're changing with it. "Technology is not neutral. We're inside of what we make, and it's inside of us. We're living in a world of connections - and it matters which ones get made and unmade."[2] What better than a collection of terms to posit discussion around what we're becoming and what we're living in? "The cyborg age is here and now, everywhere there's a car or a phone or a VCR." Haraway's most famous essay, *A Cyborg Manifesto*, broke onto the global intellectual scene in 1985 with its radical views on technology and humanity. Since then, the term cyborg has not lost its hold on the popular imagination. In addition to her work, for decades now, the idea of a machine/human construct has been prevalent in science fiction with the increase in our entanglement with technology, networks and systems of information.

When I began exploring the nascent field of Cyborg Anthropology (est. 1993) I found that as technology increased in people's lives there weren't a lot of approachable words and phrases to describe what was happening. I set out to find them, and in some cases, coin them. Some phrases in this book are new, and some, until this point, have only been scattered across the web.

This book is a first step down the road of cataloguing the new interactions and experiences of the modern cyborg subject. The articles in this book are meant as a broad invitation to examine how culture, identity and humanity is changing with respect to technology, tools and methods of communication. It is impossible to represent the entire spectrum of the cyborg in one short volume. Instead, this book's main function is to operate as a mental appetizer, a conversation-starter and a jumping-off point for the imagination. It should not be regarded or examined as a critical academic treatise.

As Haraway said, "being a cyborg isn't about how many bits of silicon you have under your skin or how many prosthetics your body contains," it has to do with networks and information, and the systems that make up our lives. I encourage readers of this book to keep this in mind as they examine the world around them.

Thanks to Sheldon Renan, Andrew Warner, Maggie Wauklyn, Jon Lebkowsky, Deborah Heath and Aaron Parecki for offering advice on this short book.

References

1-2. Kunzru, Hari. (1997) You Are Cyborg. *Wired*. Retrieved May 16, 2013, from http://www.wired.com/wired/archive/5.02/ffharaway_pr.html

Cyborg

The term **cyborg** was developed by space technologists Manfred Clynes and Nathan S. Kline, in a paper called "Cyborgs and Space." This paper detailed how humans might use external systems and attachments to survive the extremely hostile environment of space travel. Clynes and Kline described cyborgs as beings that used external components to extend "the self-regulatory control function of the organism to adapt to new environments."[1]

Types of Cyborgs

Chris Gray's *Cyborg Handbook* defines two categories of cyborg technologies in relation to humans: restorative and enhanced. Restorative technologies "restore lost function, organs, and limbs."[2] Restorative cyborgs can include, but are not limited to, those with pacemakers, insulin pumps or artificial limbs. An "enhanced cyborg" describes a person with additive technologies which increase one's capacity to do something over the general norm. Many enhanced cyborgs are found in popular fiction. Some examples are Terminator, Robocop, or Star Trek's Borg collective; these fictions explore embodied technology that only a small number of beings have access to.

The issue of how far enhanced technologies should go in transforming humanity is a subject of increasing ethical debates.

Doug Englebart's "Augmenting Human Intellect" discusses machines as help for the human brain.[3] Englebart's inspiration came from a 1945 paper by Dr. Vannevar Bush's "As We May Think"[4], a paper on the extension of self, and machines as helpers for the human brain.

Clynes and Kline's definition of cyborg describes "exogenous" or external components[1], meaning that beings can still be classified as cyborgs even if they do not have internally attached components, or technology built into the body. The idea that "we are all cyborgs"[5] comes from the fact that most modern technology users are augmenting their brains by storing content and ideas outside of themselves within technology. This view most closely fits Bush and Englebart's idea of augmented human intellect.

Cyborgs and Social Networks

Cyborgs are not just about technology and humans, but networks and information. "An automated production line in a factory, an office computer network, a club's dancers, lights, and sound systems - all are cyborg constructions of people and machines."[6] Social news networks like Reddit are coming closer to resembling Star Trek's borg collective, a machine-hybrid species that rapidly assimilates new species and ideas into their own. Ideas are often so quickly absorbed by those connected to information that people can experience a kind of "microsingularity," a moment in which geographically disconnected people experience the same news within minutes. Information can spread faster on Twitter than the speed of an earthquake's shockwaves.[7] The news of Michael Jackson's death spread through many forms of media so quickly that networks around the world were slowed.[8]

M.T. Anderson's *Feed* describes a future in which everyone's brain is physically connected to a global network of information. The book explores the drawbacks of an augmentative cyborg technology pushed to an extreme. Though the "Feed" allows people to quickly purchase items and adapt to fast-moving trends, those without access to the latest technology are stuck with ill-fitting prosthetics that remove their ability to function on the same level as their peers.

Cyborg pioneers Steve Mann[9], Neil Harbinson[10] and experimental artist Stellarc brought wider attention to cyborg technology to augment one's own experience of reality. Mann and collaborator James Fung developed wearable technology to block advertisements from reality. Colorblind artist Neil Harbinson, who normally can only see shades of grey, helped develop technology that allowed him to "hear color." Stellarc created a 3rd arm for himself, showing that technology could add to how he worked.

References

1. Clynes, Manfred E. and Nathan S. Kline, (September 1960) Cyborgs and Space. In Gray, Mentor, and Figueroa-Sarriera (Eds.), *The Cyborg Handbook*, (pp. 26-27 and 74-75) New York: Routledge.

2. Gray, Chris Hables, ed. (1995) *The Cyborg Handbook.* New York: Routledge.

3. Engelbart, Doug. (October 1962) Augmenting Human Intellect: A Conceptual Framework. *Doug Engelbart Institute.* Retrieved January 2013, from http://www.dougengelbart.org/pubs/augment-3906.html

4. Bush, Vannevar. (July 1945) As We May Think. *The Atlantic.* Retrieved January 2013, from http://www.theatlantic.com/magazine/archive/1945/07/as-we-may-think/303881/

5-6. Kunzru, Hari. (1997) You Are Cyborg. *Wired.* Retrieved May 16, 2013, from http://www.wired.com/wired/archive/5.02/ffharaway_pr.html

7. Lehmann, Sune. (August 24, 2011) TweetQuake. *Complexity and Social Networks Blog, Institute for Quantitative Social Science and the Program on Networked Governance, Harvard University.* Retrieved February 17, 2013, from http://blogs.iq.harvard.edu/netgov/2011/08/tweetquake.html

8. Shiels, Maggie. (June 26, 2009) Web slows after Jackson's death. *BBC News.* Retrieved February 17, 2013, from http://news.bbc.co.uk/2/hi/technology/8120324.stm

9. See entry on Steve Mann

10. See entry on Synesthesia

Affective Computing

Affective Computing is a term used to describe the process of using technology to help measure and communicate emotion. The concept of Affective Computing was popularized by Rosalind Picard[1], who currently runs the Affective Computing group at MIT's Media Lab.[2]

An early example of an emotionally intelligent agent is *Eliza*, one of the very first artificially intelligent chatbot programs. Eliza was written at MIT by Joseph Weizenbaum around 1966; it ran a series of psychotherapeutic scripts that provided non-judgemental feedback to questions posed by users[3]. Portland programmer Brennan Novak's project Emoome prompts the user to share their emotional state and then visualizes it for the user. This "emotional journal" enables one to look back on words and phrases associated with feelings over time.[4]

MIT Media Lab Student Kelly Dobson built a blender that operated based on the intensity of her voice.[5] Rather than saying "Blender, ON!" or pressing a button, Dobson simply made blending noises. A low-pitched "Rrrrrrrrr" turned the blender on low. If she wanted to increase the speed of the machine, she increased her voice to "RRRRRRRRRRR!" By bypassing interfaces modeled on physical buttons or terminal commands, Dobson's blender exemplified the notion that machines could also be built to take completely different types of inputs.

Projects such as the Smart Phone Frequent EDA Event Logger (FEEL) utilize a wristband sensor that measures electrodermal activity (EDA). The wristband sensor responds to stress, anxiety, and arousal to help people determine which "emails, phone calls, or meetings cause wearers the most stress or anxiousness."[6] The pocket-sized digital Tamagochi pet is another example of a device "built for affective human-computer communication."[7]

References

1. Picard, Rosalind. (2000) *Affective Computing.* Cambridge: MIT Press.

2. Highlighted Projects. *MIT Media Lab: Affective Computing Group.* Retrieved May 5, 2013, from http://affect.media.mit.edu/projects.php

3. Weizenbaum, J. (1966) ELIZA - A computer program for the study of natural language communication between man and machine. In Communications of the ACM (pp. 9(1):36-45). New York: ACM.

4. Novak, Brennan. *Emoome - Visualize Your Emotions.* Retrieved May 7, 2013, from https://emoo.me/

5. Dobson, Kelly. (2003-2004) Blendie. *MIT Media Lab.* Retrieved July 2, 2011, from http://web.media.mit.edu/~monster/blendie/

6. Ayzenberg, Yadid and Rosalind W. Picard. Smart Phone Frequent EDA Event Logger (FEEL). *MIT Media Lab: Affective Computing Group.* Retrieved May 7, 2013, from http://affect.media.mit.edu/projects.php?id=3312

7. Affective Communication. *MIT Media Lab: Affective Computing Group.* Retrieved May 5, 2013, from http://affect.media.mit.edu/projects.php

Ambient Awareness

Ambient awareness is a way of describing the idea of being cognizant of another's actions, thoughts and experiences without having to be near them physically, and without specifically requesting such information.

A child in its mother's womb receives nourishment without having to take action. This same dynamic grows more prevalent for adults with the mass adoption of the smartphone. As we move through time and space, we can increasingly access social and entertainment sentience via a single device. Our devices and surroundings have become a sort of technosocial womb. In her book *Alone Together*, Sherry Turkle describes that even when we are alone, we can feel connected through technology.

User experience designer Leisa Reichelt coined the term "Ambient Awareness" to describe how Mobile devices help us experience a kind of persistent connectedness. "It's not that we're always connected," write Reichelt, "but that we always have an ability to connect."[1] Reichelt uses the phrase "continual partial friendship"[2] to describe a feeling of loose affiliation that results from being on mobile devices. Blogger Johnnie Moore wrote that "it's not about being poked and prodded, it's about exposing more surface area for others to connect with."[3]

Futurist Alex Soojung-Kim Pang likens ambient information to "a 'type of E.S.P.,' ...an invisible dimension floating over everyday life...."[4]

One of the things essential to being a cyborg is a higher level of connectivity. Technology writer and filmmaker Sheldon Renan calls this new form of connectivity "loosely but deeply entangled."[5] We are beginning to see a new sense of time; a Collective Now, says Renan.[6]

Related Reading

"Companion Species" on page 29
"Connective Obligation" on page 31

References

1. Reichelt, L. (March 1, 2007) Disambiguity. *Leisa Reichelt's Professional Blog.* Retrieved January 2011, from http://www.disambiguity.com/ambient-intimacy/

2. Charman-Anderson S. (October 4, 2007) *Corante.* Retrieved October 2011, from http://strange.corante.com/2007/10/04/fowa07b-leisa-reichelt

3. Moore, Johnnie. (May 5, 2007) Missing the Point of Twitter. *Johnnie Moore's Weblog.* Retrieved April 7, 2011, from http://www.johnniemoore.com/blog/archives/001752.php

4. Thompson, C. (September 7, 2008) Brave New World of Digital Intimacy. *New York Times.* Retrieved April 7, 2011, from http://www.nytimes.com/2008/09/07/magazine/07awareness-t.html

5-6. Renan, Sheldon. (June 19, 2009) The Next Moore's Law - Netness: Why Everything Wants To Be Connected. Presented by Sheldon Renan at Open Source Bridge unconference session. Retrieved February 19, 2013, from http://www.slideshare.net/brampitoyo/the-next-moores-law-netness-why-everything-wants-to-be-connected

Anomie

Anomie describes a sense of disconnectedness from others in a society or community and lack of access to the ability to have impact on the community around oneself.

Sociologist Émile Durkheim popularized the term anomie in his 1897 book *Suicide*, a study of the emerging industrial society in America. Durkheim noticed that during rapid industrialization, many individuals did not feel connected to jobs, community, purpose, or life goals. The rise of modern labor forced many individuals to take jobs that were just as mechanical as the evolving environment around them. The mismatch between job and purpose made it difficult for individuals to achieve their goals.[1]

Modern society suffers from the same problems of anomie that Durkheim identified. Factory workers whose families lead agrarian lifestyles are prone to feelings of anomie due to inhospitable work environments and limited access to family.[2] Recent college graduates may have a difficult time finding jobs in the area they are interested in, and rising costs of tuition drive their need to take any job possible. Divesting goals from near-term needs creates a mismatch that can lead to loneliness, frustration and isolation.

Highways and airport could be considered temporary sources of anomie. French anthropologist Marc Augé coined the term "non-place" for spaces like these. "If a place can be defined as relational, historical and concerned with identity," wrote Augé, "then a space which cannot be defined as relational, or historical, or concerned with identity will be a non-place."[3] In spaces where connectedness lies elsewhere, the Internet or cell phone can function as an oasis. Everything wants to be connected.[4] For life, connectivity in some form facilitates survival, while isolation results in death.

References

1. Durkheim, Emile (1897) [1951]. *Suicide: a study in sociology.* The Free Press. P. 15.

2. Malone, Andrew and Jones, Richard (December 6, 2010) Revealed: Inside the Chinese Suicide Sweatshop Where Workers Toil in 34-Hour Shifts To Make Your iPod. *Daily Mail.* Retrieved February 7, 2012, from http://www.dailymail.co.uk/news/article-1285980/Revealed-Inside-Chinese-suicide-sweatshop-workers-toil-34-hour-shifts-make-iPod.html

3. Marc Augé, (1995) *Non-Places: Introduction to an Anthropology of Supermodernity.* London & New York: Verso Books. Pp. 77-78

4. Renan, Sheldon. (June 19, 2009) The Next Moore's Law - Netness: Why Everything Wants To Be Connected. Presented by Sheldon Renan at Open Source Bridge unconference session. Retrieved February 19, 2013, from http://www.slideshare.net/brampitoyo/the-next-moores-law-netness-why-everything-wants-to-be-connected

Architecture Fiction

Architecture fiction is a way of exploring and testing alternatively-built forms and urban environments without the overhead of physically building and testing objects in real life. Bruce Sterling coined the term after reading J. G. Ballard's *A Handful of Dust*[1] (an essay published by the Guardian about modernist architecture) to suggest that it is possible to write fiction with architecture.[2]

Fictional narratives allow one to enter safely into an alternate world and explore possible effects of a slightly different system or ruleset. Unlike architects, a writer does not require fundraising, grants or permission to simulate possible futures or explore alternate timelines and histories.

Cultural critic Mark Dery wrote "architecture fiction anticipates the future present,"[3] and Sterling added "the field becomes almost infinitely more exciting when you realize that architectural projects, by definition, entail the reimagination of how humans might inhabit the earth," and architecture fiction can explore how humans "organize themselves spatially and give shape to their everyday lives."[4]

Bruce Sterling's *The Growthing* is an example of architecture fiction by Bruce Sterling.[5] Other examples include work from the Hypothetical Development Organization, which invents a "hypothetical future for each selected structure"[6] starting with a number of fictional plans for developments in New Orleans. Designer and filmmaker Keiichi Matsuda's work explores aspects of augmented reality in the urban experience.

References

1. Ballard, JG. (March 19, 2006) A Handful of Dust. *The Guardian.* Retrieved June 2011, from http://www.guardian.co.uk/artanddesign/2006/mar/20/architecture.communities

2. Varnelis, K. (March 2, 2009) In Defense of Architecture. *Varnelis.net.* Retrieved January 2011, from http://varnelis.net/topics_115

3. Dery, Mark. (February 9, 2011) Architecture Fiction: Premonitions of the Present. *Thought Catalog.* Retrieved June 2011, from http://thoughtcatalog.com/2011/architecture-fiction-premonitions-of-the-present

4. Sterling, Bruce. (December 31, 2008) BLDGBLOG enters 2009. *WIRED Magazine.* http://www.wired.com/beyond_the_beyond/2008/12/bldgblog-enters/

5. Sterling, Bruce. (January 2003) The Growthing. *Metropolismag.com.* Retrieved March 2013, from http://www.metropolismag.com/html/content_0103/str/

6. The Hypothetical Development Organization. Retrieved March 2013, from http://hypotheticaldevelopment.com/about.html

Asynchronous Communication

Asynchronous communication describes the act of communicating with another person by posting messages through a medium that stores communication in external devices such as phones, text, or letters. Asynchronous communication arose when humans began to externalize memories through cave painting and writing.

Asynchronous communication is different from synchronous communication because the latter is concerned with messages that are sent and received in real time. Asynchronous communication can be carried out over long periods of time through networks of letters or the sharing of moments on personal devices, while synchronous tools enable real-time communication and collaboration in a "same time different place" mode[1].

The growth of network technology available to society leads to an increasing number of ways to carry out asynchronous communication can be carried out. Though some individuals expect almost immediate responses in technologically-mediated interactions, asynchronous communication remains essential for some activities, especially as groups interact across time zones.

Asynchronous communication can be useful for one-to-many communications, remote teaching, commenting and feedback, and coordinating personal or business schedules.

Asynchronous social networks such as Twitter allow for one-to-one or one-to-many communications. This is especially convenient for celebrities, as one-to-many social network make it possible to communicate with fans in a way that was not previously possible.[2]

References

1. Ashley, Julia. Synchronous and Asynchronous Communication Tools. *Asae Center*. Retrieved January 2013, from http://www.asaecenter.org/Resources/articledetail.cfm?itemnumber=13572

2. Alice Marwick and danah boyd (2011) To See and Be Seen: Celebrity Practice. In J. Knight, A. Weedon (Eds.) *Convergence: The International Journal of Research into New Media Technologies* (pp. 148). New York: Sage Publications.

Celebrity as Cyborg

The **celebrity** is the ultimate form of cyborg, existing in an network of participants and creators attached to a system of production, reproduction and distribution. The celebrity is an example of the creation of identity through technology. A digital celebrity symbiotically produces, distributes and advertises with its audience. Instead of a publicist or agent managing their words, a celebrity can directly communicate in an intimate manner with many fans at once.

Celebrities consist of carefully constructed moments augmented by makeup, lighting, and video. The celebrity cannot be fully consumed, and thus the more times the viewer accesses the celebrity, the more their mental taste buds seek new celebrity data.

Identity Production

The process that produces the celebrity is made up of many team members, each having expertise in a specific area: hairstylists and producers, creative directors and billboard designers, agents, filmmakers and directors, advertisers and salespeople. The other part of the network are the viewers. Both technology and humans are a part of the same symbiotic netowork of actors. Non-human actors in the network are exemplified in Callon and Latour's theory of actors and networks.[1] Fans do not see the unprocessed human at any moment but form parasocial relationships: viewers know a great deal about the celebrity, but the celebrity is minimally aware or knows little to nothing about their fans.[2]

Digital Celebrity

Celebrities on social networks create a sense of intimacy in the digital space. One can almost feel like they are hanging out the celebrity on Twitter or Facebook, creating a feeling of knowing them.[3] For celebrities on the social network Twitter, each tweet is a continual production and management of identity. "...tweets serve a social function, reinforcing connections and maintaining social bonds."[4]

References

1. Latour, B. (2005) *Reassembling the Social: An Introduction to Actor-Network-Theory.* Oxford: Oxford University Press.

2. Horton, Donald; R. Richard Wohl (1956) Mass communication and para-social interaction: Observations on intimacy at a distance. Psychiatry 19 (3): 215–229. PMID 13359569. republished in Particip@tions 3 (1) ISSN 1749-8716

3. Alice Marwick and danah boyd (2011) To See and Be Seen: Celebrity Practice. In J. Knight, A. Weedon (Eds.) *Convergence: The International Journal of Research into New Media Technologies* (pp. 148). New York: Sage Publications.

4. Crawford K (2009) These foolish things: On Intimacy and Insignificance in Mobile Media. In G. Goggin and L. Hjorth (Eds.) *Mobile Technologies: From Telecommunications to Media* (pp. 252-265). New York: Routledge.

City as Software

City as Software is the idea that a city is a system capable of being edited by its citizens. Urban theorist Adam Greenfield wrote that viewing a city as software allows for citizens to engage and co-author the environment they inhabit in a fundamentally new way.[1]

The idea behind a City as Software is that the city evolves through errors that are detected and corrected by everyday citizens, instead of a handful of people employed on behalf of the city. Some cities are beginning to provide open data sets that allow citizens to interface with the city's urban information and are encouraging developers to build applications on top of it.

Some cities provide Application Programming Interfaces, or APIs, to their citizens. An API gives applications easier access to formatted data. Open data advocate Max Ogden worked on an API for the City of Portland, Oregon called PDXAPI. The API consolidated and standardized multiple civic datasets into a single resource so that the data could be easily used by developers. In a 2011 presentation on open government, Ogden pointed out that while governments are good at providing data, they are not well-suited to creating interfaces for that data. Thus, a government's job should be to provide open data, and a citizen's job should be to make it usable by anyone through the creation of apps built on that data.[2]

One of Ogden's apps, "Portland Smells," allowed citizens to geotag and report smells around the city. After citizens began reporting smells all over Portland, the city commissioned Ogden to build another version of the app that allowed citizens to report toxic smells. This helped the city to isolate and identify toxic spills and environmental issues that individual city inspectors didn't have the resources to measure.

Related Reading

"Architecture Fiction" on page 21
"Equipotential Space" on page 41
"Mundane Studies" on page 65

References

1. Greenfield, A. (July 7, 2010) Frameworks for Citizen Responsiveness: Towards a Read/Write Urbanism. *Urban Omnibus.* Retrieved July 2010, from http://urbanomnibus.net/2010/07/frameworks-for-citizen-responsiveness-towards-a-readwrite-urbanism/

2. Ogden, Max. (2011) Why Middleware is the Key to a Successful Gov 2.0. *GOSCON 2011.* Retrieved December 2011, from http://goscon.org/ignitespeakers

Companion Species

The concept of a **companion species** has been around for hundreds of years. Humans did not evolve by themselves. We co-evolved alongside animals.

Animals are one companion species. Technology is another. Cyborg scholar Donna Haraway first connected the concept of a companion species to technology in the late 90's. Haraway used the term as an exploration of the emergence of animals who are not meat animals, lab animals, wilderness animals, war dogs, vermin or pariah dogs, but who are part of a very particular historical relationship.[1]

In her *Companion Species Manifesto*, Haraway considers "dogs as the most significant example of companion species, the cyborg being but a toddler in our world of interspecies relations."[2]

The concept of a companion species isn't limited to animals or even to living things. Cell phones, for example, could be considered a companion species. They cry, and must be picked up. They are hungry, and must be plugged into a wall at night to be fed. They must be upgraded, protected, and cared for. In return, they provide information, connectivity and entertainment. They grow alongside humans and adapt to fit our needs, as humans simultaneously adapt to fit the needs of the device.

References

1. Haraway, Donna. (August 2000) Birth of the Kennel: A Lecture by Donna Haraway. *The European Graduate School.* Retrieved June 2010, from http://www.egs.edu/faculty/donna-haraway/articles/birth-of-the-kennel/

2. Boulanger, Julie. (May 2004) Review of the The Companion Species Manifesto by Donna Haraway. *Bookslut.* Retrieved October 2011, from http://www.bookslut.com/nonfiction/2004_05_002059.php

Connective Obligation

When one can access information anywhere, at any point in the day, one may increasingly feel the need to stay "always on." When phones were limited to rooms and limited to cords, one could only respond to phone calls where a landline was available. Now that consumer devices allow people to communicate anywhere, many may feel obligated to respond to important messages or emails in any place and at any time. Should the message arrive when the person is not connected, feelings of guilt may arise.

Cell phone researcher Richard Ling studied feelings of obligation in teenagers whose use of phones was a part of everyday life. Ling found that "during the focus groups, teens related many stories of friends and acquaintances who get insulted, angry or upset if a text message or phone call is not responded to immediately," and that "as a result, many teens we heard from said they feel obligated to return texts and calls as quickly as possible."[1] One high school girl explained:

> "That is one aggravating thing I find about phones…when it gets to the point where you can receive like all your messages and all this, then you have no way of disconnecting. That didn't used to bother me until on a family vacation, my uncle, the entire time typing his emails, doing his business. It's like, 'Why is it so hard for you to put that away for one day [and enjoy family meal?]' "[2]

At the end of several of the focus groups, participants were asked to share with the group what they thought were the best and worst things about having a cell phone. Ling found that a small number of adolescents managed others' expectations by simply limiting their availability. One boy explained that he was "bad at answering my cell phone," and that he would, "just leave it on the counter and walk somewhere else and come back and see a missed call. So people expect that from me. They don't expect necessarily a quick answer."[3]

References

1-3. Ling, Richard, Amanda Lenhart, Scott Campbell and Kristen Purcell. (April 20, 2010) Teens and Mobile Phones. *Pew Internet and American Life Project.* Retrieved April 20, 2011, from http://www.pewinternet.org/Reports/2010/Teens-and-Mobile-Phones/Chapter-3/Feeling-obligated-to-stay-connected.aspx

Cyborg Security

The extension of the self brings with it an entire new dimension of security concerns. **Cyborg Security** is a phrase used to describe a set of practices and tools for protecting the extended self and its data. With the advent of social media, online banking and payments, cloud storage, and smartphones, keeping one's data and identity protected becomes increasingly important.

Stolen or compromised identity is an increasingly dangerous issue given the fact that so many identities are shared across multiple social platforms. Having access to one's Gmail or Facebook account can allow someone to log in to any other social network and if not caught quickly can lead to a compromised reputation among other things. Researcher danah boyd* discovered that some teenagers disable their Facebook accounts when they go offline to prevent people from posting on their wall when they're not there to "defend" it. This practice, also known as "super-logoff"[1] is an example of a risk reduction strategy cyborg selves.

Portland entrepreneur Ken Westin created GadgetTrak software that allows users to remotely track and recover stolen laptops and mobile devices. Other security software features include remote wiping of stolen machines or alarms if devices are moved too far away from their owners.

Entire countries' Twitter accounts have been taken over, for example when Anonymous took over North Korea's Twitter and Flickr accounts changing pro-North-Korean propaganda into a criticism of nuclear weapons.[2]

Misinformation from accounts can lead to dangerous situations. On April 23, 2013, the Associated Press Twitter account was hacked. The attacker posted false claims of explosions at the White House. Associates were quick to debunk the false news before it spread, but it could have resulted in a panic if not properly debunked.[3]

References

1. boyd, danah*. (November 8, 2010) Risk Reduction Strategies on Facebook. *Zephoria.org.* Retrieved June 5, 2011, from http://www.zephoria.org/thoughts/archives/2010/11/08/risk-reduction-strategies-on-facebook.html

* danah boyd chooses not to capitalize her name. Her name is legally danah michele boyd. You can read more about danah's name and her decisions behind it at http://www.danah.org/name.html

2. Brodkin, Jon. (April 4, 2013) Anonymous hackers take control of North Korean propaganda accounts. *ArsTechnica.* Retrieved May 2013, from http://arstechnica.com/security/2013/04/anonymous-hackers-take-control-of-north-korean-propaganda-sites/

3. Welch, Chris. (April 23, 2013) AP Twitter account hacked, makes false claim of explosions at White House. *The Verge.* Retrieved May 2013, from http://www.theverge.com/2013/4/23/4257392/ap-twitter-hacked-claims-explosions-white-house-president-injured

Digital Backyard

Digital backyard is a term used to describe the transition of exploratory youth culture from the analog backyard space to digital space. This is a tendency brought on by the fact that many families live in smaller spaces with less backyard space, spread out by geographic distance from friends. These children's virtual playgrounds "are huge and universal [while] at the same time they shrink the world to a tiny space with the point of a mouse, the click of a button."[1]

Playing together online in a distributed social network is a new form of backyard play. In digital backyard play, children explore the extents and limits and offerings of a digital space vs. the analog space. Children's environments are no longer restricted to only outdoor and the indoor home, school and the local, but now include the virtual and significantly more of the global.[2] The new connected adolescence uses existing structures and experiments with them. Virtual worlds allow children to come together from geographically dispersed backgrounds to worldwide virtual foregrounds, transcending geographical barriers not only to play and communicate but also to collaborate, corroborate and express in a whole new way.[3] By going above and beyond to connect in new ways or use existing structures for humorous games, this generation challenges each other in the digital space with pranks and challenges. Through these games, they learn how to push each other's limits, understand what their own bodies can do, and how to experience danger and excitement. These new worlds allow children to play across nation states without passports, travel, or language.

Minecraft, an independent game released in 2009, allows anyone to build anything they like in a virtual environment full of blocks. Minecraft is an "open world" game that allows people from all over the world to meet and build together, or build alone. Unlike the real world, Minecraft provides almost unlimited virtual space for a multitude of creations. The environment is accessible to almost anyone with a computer, and has become very popular with people of all ages, especially children. Many view it as "a newer, less expensive LEGO set,"[4] where blocks are unlimited and never run out.

References

1-3. De Lange, Magda. (March 29, 2012) An analysis of the virtual world ClubPenguin.com. *Interdisciplinary Child Studies*. Retrieved December 29, 2012, from http://magdachildstudies.blogspot.com/2012/03/analysis-of-virtual-world-club-penguin.html

4. Luke Plunkett. (February 5, 2013) A Short, But Wonderful Documentary About Why Kids Play Minecraft. *Kotaku*. Retrieved June 2013, from http://kotaku.com/5981660/a-short-but-wonderful-documentary-about-why-kids-play-minecraft

Digital Hoarding

Digital hoarding is a term used to describe the act of hoarding material or information in some type of digital format.

Analog hoarding is physically noticeable. Individuals with hoarding disorders have found themselves physically suffocated or trapped underneath piles of newspapers.[1] Individuals may hoard hundreds of cats or other animals, and keep every piece of trash within the walls of their home.

Digital hoarding behaviors may not be easily detected or treated as physical hoarding, because it is a "practice that is more hidden than physical hoarding."[2] Unlike hoarding in real life, digital hoarding may be done anywhere one has access to a phone or computer. A person sitting in a coffeeshop may be compulsively saving photos or news stories, or hoarding items on social bulletin boards like Pinterest without anyone around them noticing.

Digital artifacts do not take up any physical space. This allows one to add more and more information to a hard drive, server or device without it getting heavier. Digital cameras, email clients and hard drives are very easy to add information to. Online storage services make it easier to save, upload, create and store content than to review, delete or destroy that same content. These factors can quickly lead to excessive information accumulation on devices.

References

1. Hills, Suzannah. (February 2012) Compulsive hoarder, 85, freed from mountain of clutter after getting trapped under bags and boxes for 30 hours. *Daily Mail*. Retrieved March 2013, from http://www.dailymail.co.uk/news/article-2271750/Compulsive-hoarder-85-freed-mountain-clutter-getting-trapped-bags-boxes-30-HOURS.html

2. Beck, Melinda. (March 27, 2012) Drowning in Email, Photos, Files? Hoarding Goes Digital. *Wall Street Journal Health Journal.* Retrieved December 20, 2012, from http://online.wsj.com/article/SB10001424052702303404704577305520318265602.html

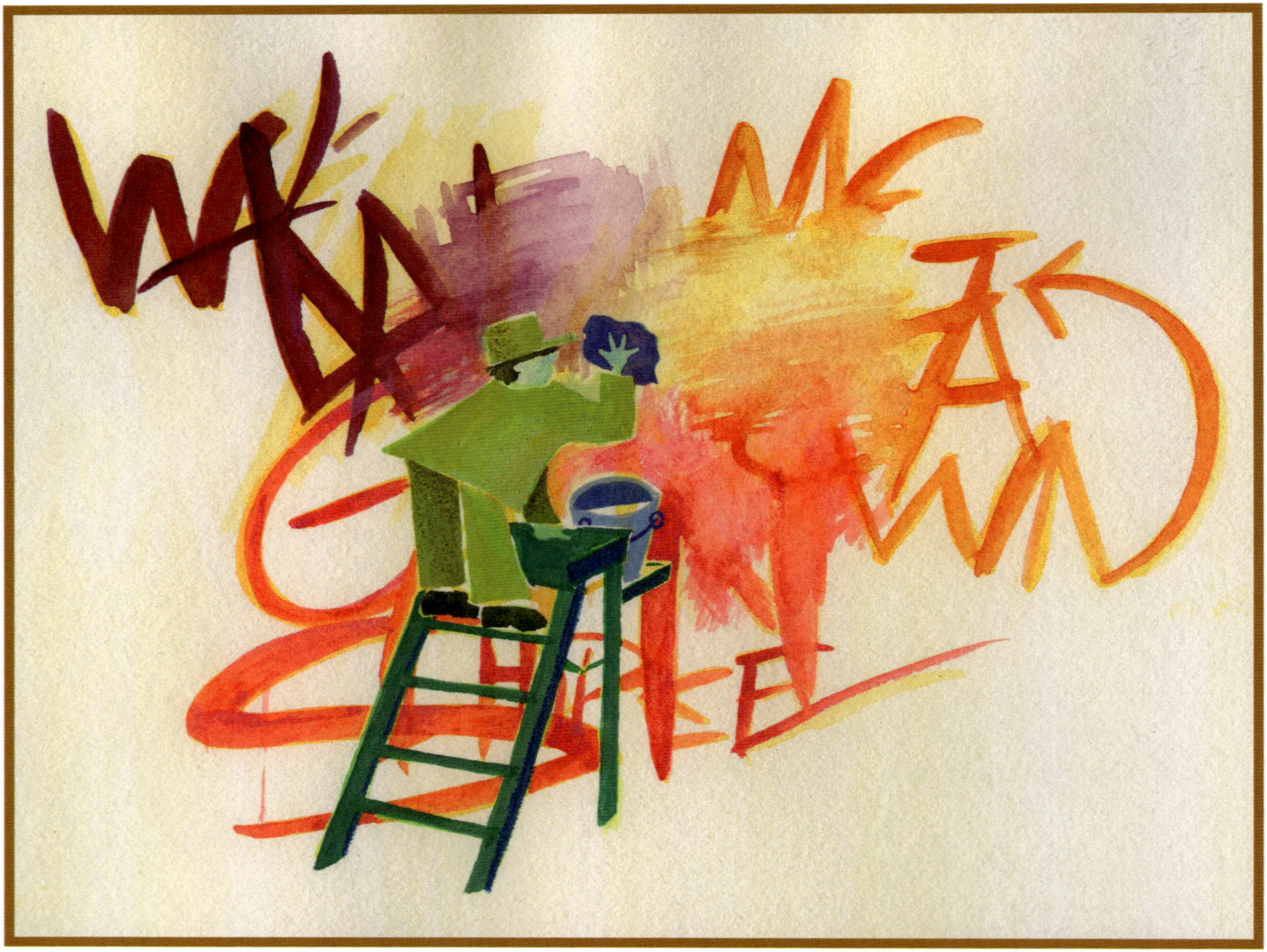

Diminished Reality

Diminished reality describes a process of blocking out real or digital information in one's reality. Unlike augmented reality, the idea of adding something to reality, diminished reality provides a kind of computer mediated reality, the ability for something to be taken away from reality rather than the ability to only add to reality. The concept of diminished reality was created by wearable computing pioneer Steve Mann and collaborators[1] to describe a method of using technology to block out undesired information from everyday life in real time.

Mann and graduate student James Fung worked on a wearable camera and monocular display called the EyeTap. One of the features of the EyeTap was that it could remove objects from video in real time and send them back to the viewer, allowing the viewer to perceive that the objects are no longer there. Mann and Fung used computer vision techniques to create a real-time billboard-blocking application. The app could block out billboards, ads and logos, and replace them with emails and text messages of the wearer's choosing. Through the aid of the EyeTap, one's reality was capable of being customized and altered. Instead of the data on street signs being owned by someone else, the EyeTap allowed one to modify, delete and customize signs and ads around them.

Humans routinely create their own diminished reality as they move through the world. One could be standing next to someone, but mentally block them out in order to not interact with them. "This allows one to find the open seat on a crowded train, or to move to the other side of the sidewalk well in advance of people handing out flyers or crappy free newspapers..."[2] Mimi Smartypants calls this concept an Urban Eye Slide, a "skill that most of us city mice have." Smartypants defines it as "the ability to scope out one's surroundings quickly but without seeming to look at anything at all." Humans have quickly learned to look only at certain portions of websites, intuitively blocking ads as they browse the web.

References

1. Mann, Steve. (May 29, 2001) Diminished Reality. *WearCam.org.* Retrieved January 2011, from http://wearcam.org/diminished_reality.htm

2. Smartypants, Mimi. (2004) *The World According to Mimi Smartypants.* New York: Harper Collins. Pg. 9

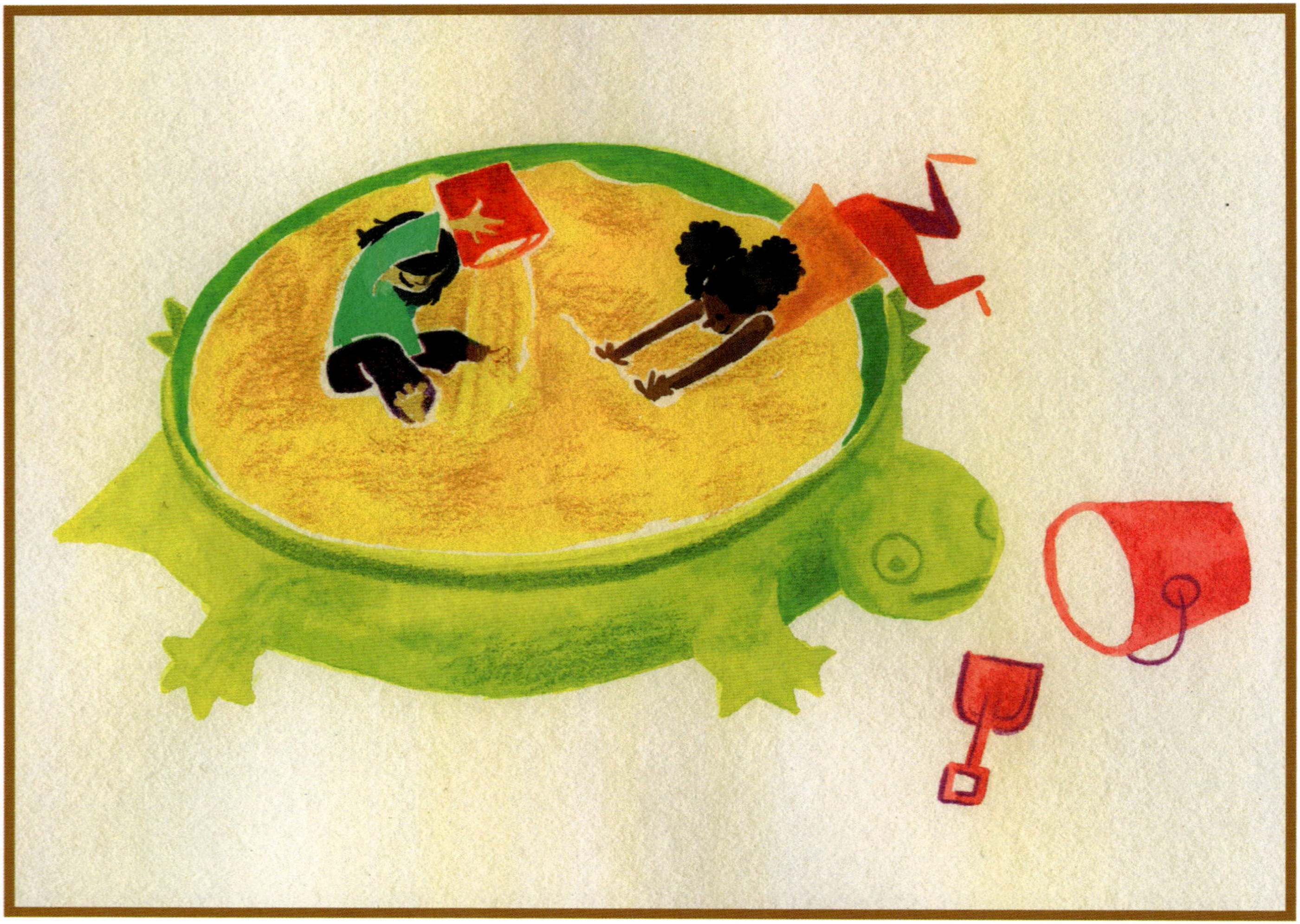

Equipotential Space

The term **Equipotential Space** was coined by Renato Serverino in 1970 in his book *Equipotential Space: Freedom in Architecture.*

Serverino described Equipotential Space as space that has the potential to be anything at any time. He wrote that, "Instead of being planned for a few specific purposes, Equipotential Space can be modulated at will for any purpose."[1] Many architectural theorists during the late 1960s and early 1970s conceptualized these types of "future spaces." Some architects even attempted to create modular futuristic spaces that could deform at will, each resembling spaceships, pods, or interlocking pieces suited for one to many occupants. "Equipotential Space offers the possibility of real freedom," wrote Serverino, "This is not freedom just to be different, but freedom to participate as fully as possible, given social, economic and technical reality."[2]

While the theories and manifestos of Serverino did not play out in the physical world of architecture and construction, they were harbingers of a new era of that invisible space between machines. Serverino's book was about the future of physical architecture, but it describes the form of the Internet perfectly. It is quite costly to create a persistently livable space whose form and function differ based on its users. In contrast, the Internet is an Equipotential space by definition, as it is comprised of fluid, editable code and the spaces between networked machines.

The digital architecture of online communities and networked spaces have shown us a full realization of Severino's Equipotential Space. These sites provide us with, as Serverino wrote, the "freedom to shape responsive solutions to immediate needs; and when these needs change, to have a new solution."[3] Just as people consciously create the shape of networks through programming and design, the shape of networks affect how people interact and behave.

References

1. Severino, Renato. (1970) Equipotential Space: Freedom in Architecture. New York: Praeger Publishers. Pg. 14.

2-3. Severino, Renato. (1970) Equipotential Space: Freedom in Architecture. New York: Praeger Publishers. Pg. 29.

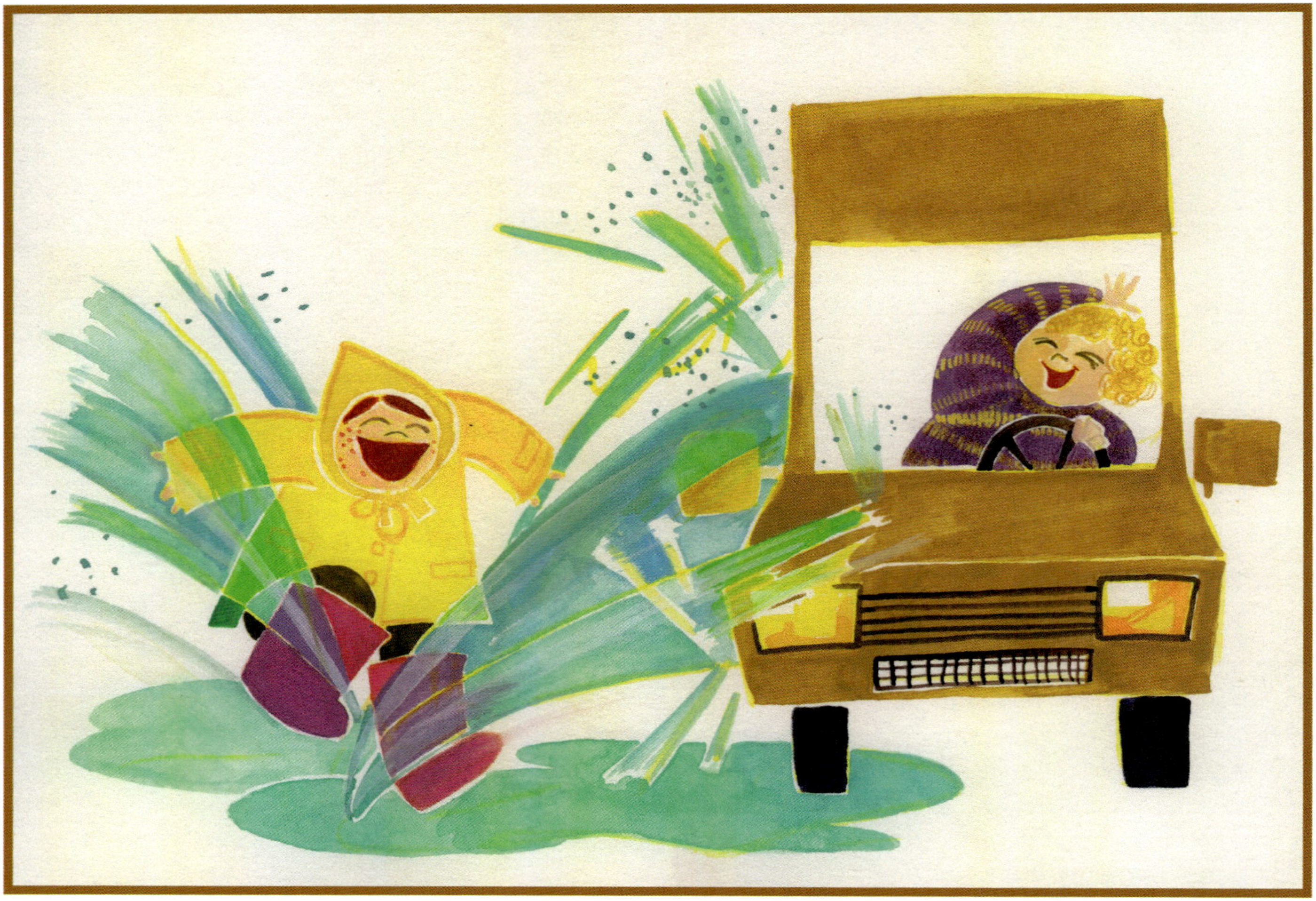

Extended Nervous System

Extended Nervous System is a term used to describe the extension of perception and sensory feedback outside the physical body.

A study on monkeys and tool use led by neuroscientist Giacomo Rizzolatti of the University of Parma in Italy suggests that the brain treats tools as just another body part.[1] Humans and vehicles behave in the same way. When one enters a vehicle, perception and sense of self automatically extend to the edges of the vehicle. The vehicle's edges are an extension of the self, and the vehicle itself is an extension of the foot.[2]

The extended nervous system does not just relate to the extension of the physical self, but the extension of the mental self as well. "At a fundamental level, physiological computing represents an extension of the human nervous system," writes Steve Fairclough. "This is nothing new. Our history is littered with tools and artifacts, from the plough to the internet, designed to extend the 'reach' of human sense capabilities. As our technology becomes more compact, we become increasingly reliant on tools to augment our cognitive capacity."[3]

Social networks are a natural extension of the social and mental self. Each user extends part of their identity into virtual space, and when that extended self is accessed, a feedback loop occurs. Getting a comment on a blog post or piece of writing becomes the psychological equivalent of receiving a comment in real life. System administrators and ops technicians have extended nervous systems that encompass the status of the systems they maintain. Having a site crash is like suddenly losing command of a body part.

References

1. Balter, Michael. (January 28, 2008) Tool Use Is Just a Trick of the Mind. *Science Now.* Retrieved May 2013, from http://news.sciencemag.org/sciencenow/2008/01/28-02.html

2. Elek, Paul. (1968) Comments and Excerpts from *Urban Structure.* New York: John Wiley & Sons, Inc. Pg. 127.

3. Fairclough, Steve. (January 6, 2010) The Extended Nervous System. *Physiological Computing.* Retrieved October 2011, from http://www.physiologicalcomputing.net/?p=291

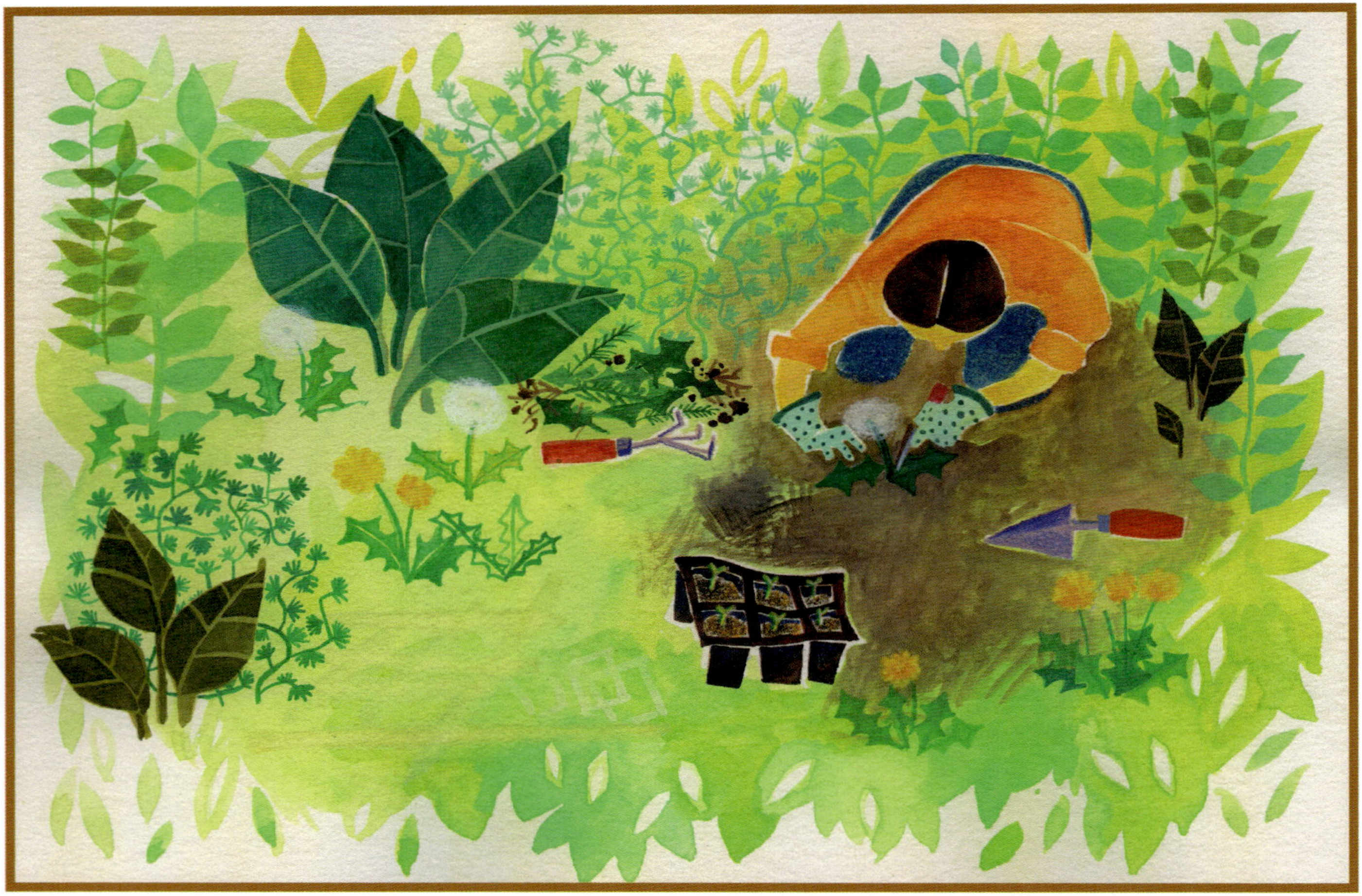

Flow

Flow describes the experience of being completely immersed in a single activity. The term was first coined by Hungarian psychology professor Mihály Csíkszentmihály to describe a feeling of "intense and focused concentration on what one is doing in the present moment, a merging of action and awareness, and an experience of activity as intrinsically rewarding."[1]

Flow involves a specific physiological feeling of being in harmony with one's tools or project, such as a computer or cell phone. In addition, those experiencing a state of flow may lose their sense of time, "typically, [experiencing] a sense that time has passed faster than normal."[2] Those experiencing a state of flow sometimes refer to it as being "in the moment" or "wired in."

The recent phenomenon of browsing Wikipedia for hours on end is an example of a "flow state."[3]

References

1-2. Csíkszentmihályi, Mihály and Jeanne Nakamura. (2001) The Concept of Flow. In C.R. Snyder and S. J. Lopez (Eds.) *The Handbook of Positive Psychology.* Oxford: Oxford University Press. Pg. 90.

3. Munroe, Randall. (February 2010) The Problem with Wikipedia. *XKCD.* Retrieved June 2013, from http://xkcd.com/214/

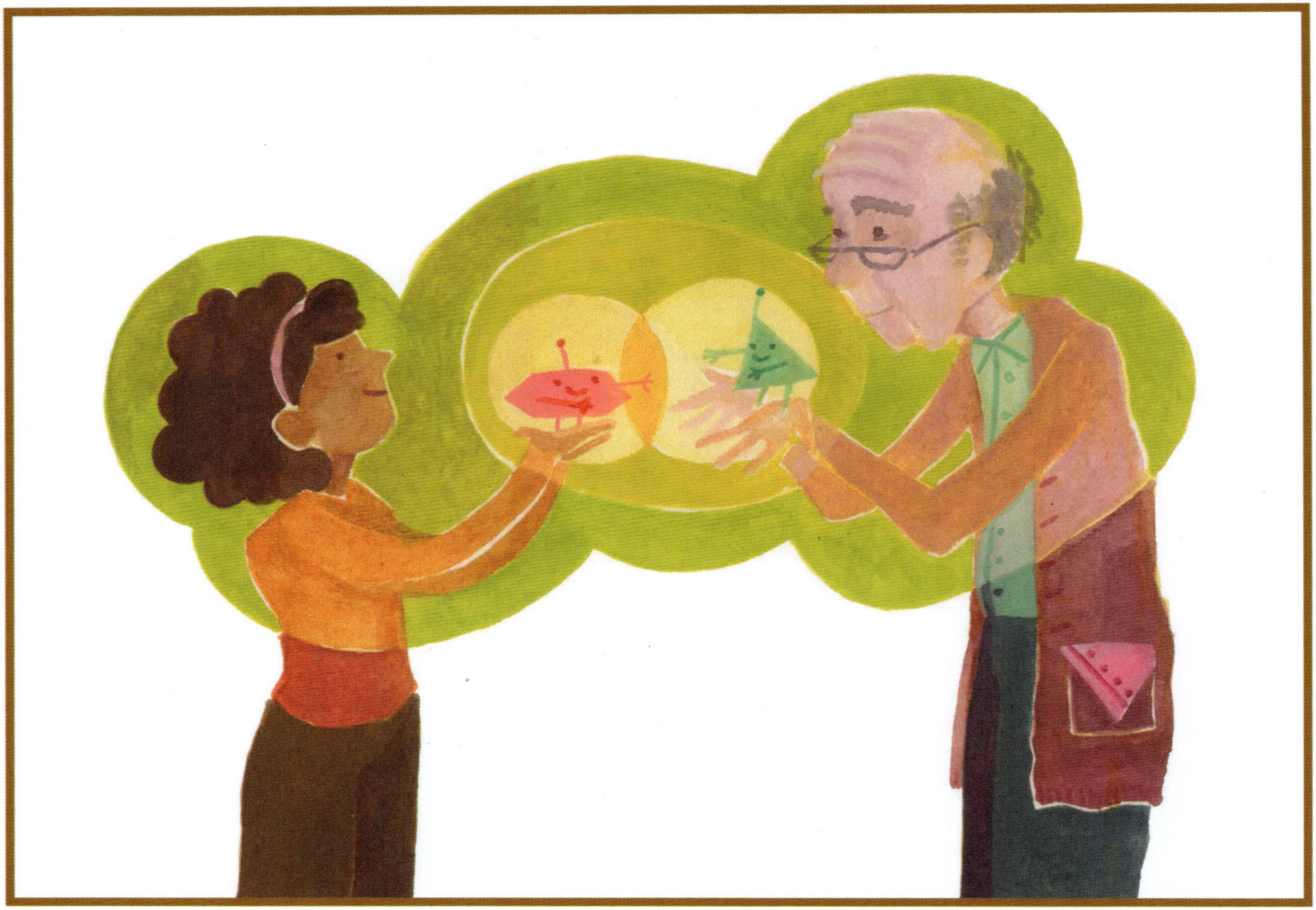

Hertzian Space

Everything that requires electricity gives off an electromagnetic field that extends into space. **Hertzian Space** is a term used to describe a holistic view of the electronic device and its cultural interactions. Hertzian space was coined by Interaction Designer Anthony Dunne and Architect Fiona Raby to describe the "electroclimate," inhabited by humans and electronic machines, as the interface between electromagnetic waves and human experiences.[1] Marisa Gómez refers to Hertzian Space as the "immaterial infrastructure that supports our current telecommunication universe."[2]

Visible light is part of Hertzian space, as well as radio, medical X-rays, television signals and UV tanning lamps. While we only see the discrete object, there is in fact an entire wave-field emanating from the object. Dunne and Raby believe that increased awareness of Hertzian space will assist our design practices. They think that we are only beginning to understand the effects and consequences of technological advances, and that "it is an environment that must be fully understood if it is to be made habitable."[3]

Media theorist Marshall McLuhan wrote that "The new media and technologies by which we amplify and extend ourselves constitute huge collective surgery carried out on the social body with complete disregard for antiseptics... For in operating on society with a new technology, it is not the incised area that is most affected... It is the entire system that is changed."[4]

Alvin Toffler's 1970 book Future Shock discussed how technology is advancing more quickly than we may be able to understand, study, or objectively look at it, pointing out that this is due to "too much change in too short a period of time."[5] Hertzian space is one of the pieces of this new reality that we exist in. Many of us no longer think of the invisible wifi and cell tower signals that tie us together.

References

1. Dunne, Anthony. (2000) *Hertzian Tales: Electronic Products, Aesthetic Experience, and Critical Design.* Cambridge: MIT Press.

2. Gómez, Marisa. (October 2011) Visualizing "Hertzian Space." *Interartive: A Platform for Contemporary Art and Thought.* Retrieved January 2013 from http://interartive.org/2011/10/hertzian-spaces-invisible-fields/

3. See ref 1.

4. McLuhan, Marshall. (1964) *Understanding Media: The Extensions of Man. 1st Ed.* New York: McGraw Hill. Pg. 70.

5. Toffler, Alvin. (1970) Future Shock. New York: Random House

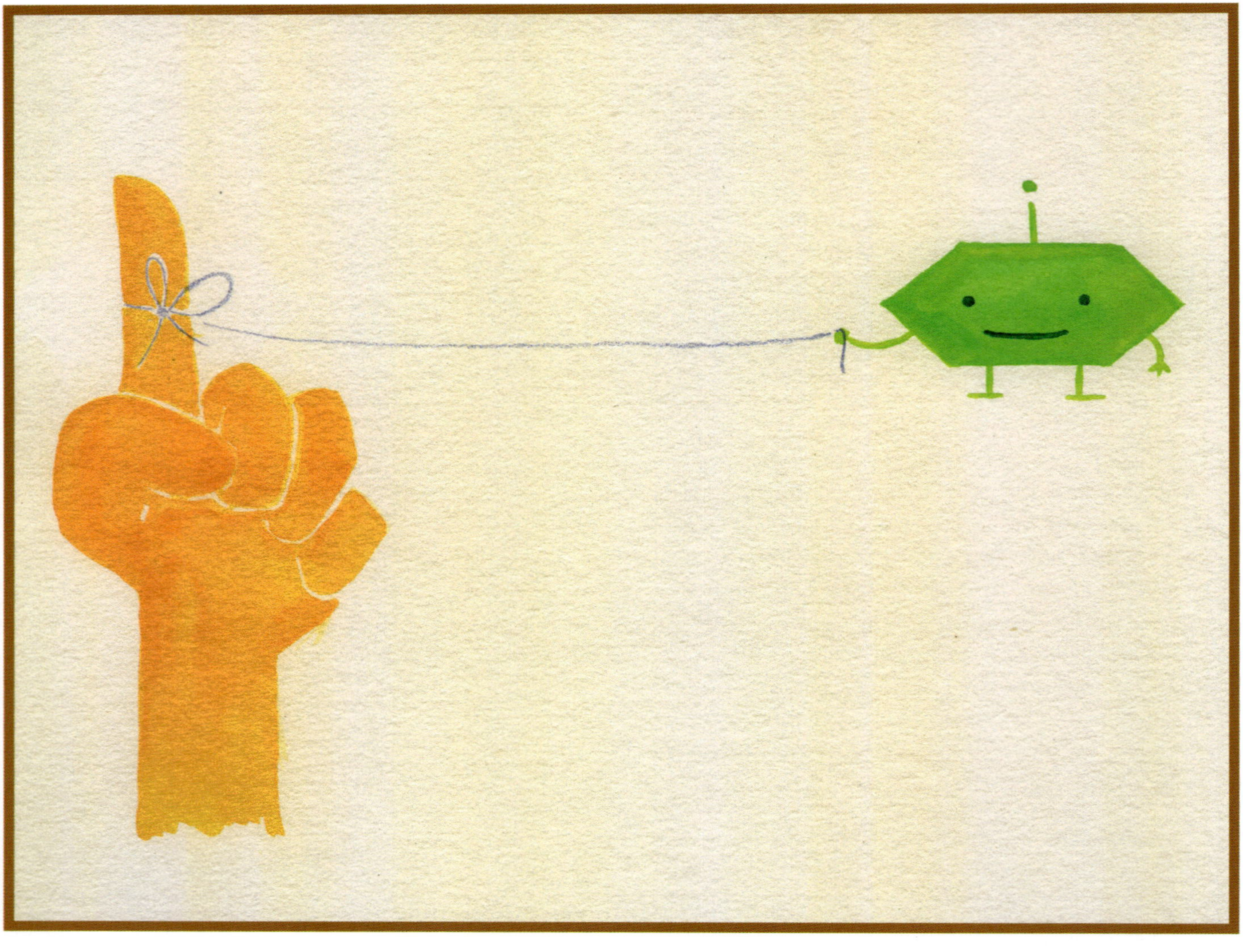

Hyperlinked Memories

Hyperlinked memories describes the idea of recalling memories through accessing information stored on computer networks. Computers provide an additional way to search through our own memories, and the collective memory of others. If we forget the location of an email or file, we can simply search for the keyword and the computer finds the file.

When we forget the location of a memory, we say it's at the "tip of the tongue." If we can remember the trigger word, then it is easy to remember the memory. On a search engine, it is possible to search the memory store of an entire collective brain simply by entering trigger words. With the help of smartphones and search engines, we can access hyperlinked memories anywhere. The transition from primarily storing information inside the brain to outside the brain means that people are increasingly remembering fewer and fewer basic facts.[1]

Anthropologist Michael Wesch noticed that the availability of memories online was beginning to change the social patterns of social storytelling. During a series of observations, he noticed that teenagers were no longer only telling stories to each other through just their voices, but were using YouTube on smartphones and laptops to tell their stories. Group members who shared the best videos gained social clout,[2] just as if they had told a successful story to their friends.

Group members who told the best stories that riffed off of the current group topic had the most clout in the situation. YouTube videos were a frequent memory store for the group members.

References

1. Your Outboard Brain Knows All. http://www.wired.com/techbiz/people/magazine/15-10/st_thompson

2. Wesch, Micheal. (July 26, 2008) An anthropological introduction to YouTube. *Library of Congress.* Retrieved October 2010, from http://www.youtube.com/watch?v=TPAO-lZ4_hU

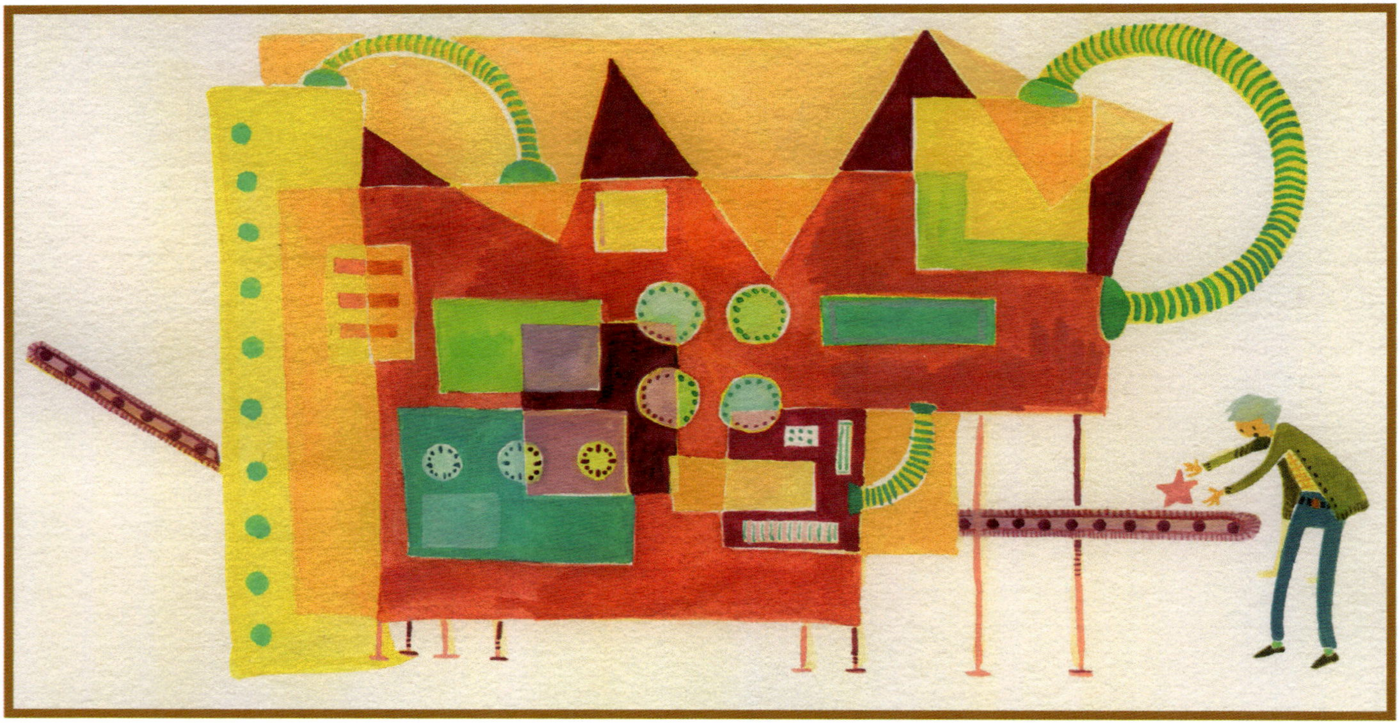

Identity Production

Identity Production is a phrase used to describe how one manages and creates an outwardly perceived self in relation to others. Identity roles are formed by individuals and given by a community.

Identity production is related to *The Presentation of Self in Everyday Life*, a seminal work by Sociologist Erving Goffman.[1] Goffman gave examples on how one's identity was reproduced daily based on situation and social relation. A person might have many identities that transition throughout the day. A person might be a father in evening, husband in the morning, and an employee or manager during the day. As Deleuze wrote in "Postscript on Societies of Control," today the self is not so much constituted by any notion of identity but rather is reduced to "dividuals."[2]

Identity can be created in many ways online, whether through text in blogs and news articles, status updates, or photos and video. As historian and architecture theorist Varnelis writes that "instead of whole individuals, we are constituted in multiple micro-publics, inhabitants of simultaneously overlapping telecocoons, sharing telepresence with intimates in whom we are in near-constant touch."[3] Some individuals curate online identity by carefully choosing which moments of their lives are shared. Others choose not filter what they post online, instead using social networks as a place for their present moments and feelings, allowing the network to be a true extension of their offline self.

Some individuals use the web try out different roles that differ from the gender, race, appearance or social class ascribed at birth. "The very idea of a 'screen name' different from one's actual-world name can imply a role"[4] Some note that although their real-world versions and identities may be very weak, they could be very strong on the web. Second Life, an online virtual world first launched in 2003 allows residents to build, fly around, and co-inhabit a world through the creation of a secondary virtual self. Some residents had separate identities online and offline. Some whose identities were strong online, may be socially anxious offline. As one Second Life resident pointed out, "the [Second Life] me and the [real life] me are two totally different people."

References

1. Goffman, Erving. (1959) *The Presentation of Self in Everyday Life.* New York: Anchor Books.

2-3. Varnelis, Kazys. (2007) The Rise of Network Culture. *Varnelis.net* Retrieved July 2011, from http://varnelis.net/the_rise_of_network_culture

3. Boellstorff, Tom. (2010) *Coming of Age in Second Life* Princeton University Press. Pg 119.

4. Ibid., Pg. 120.

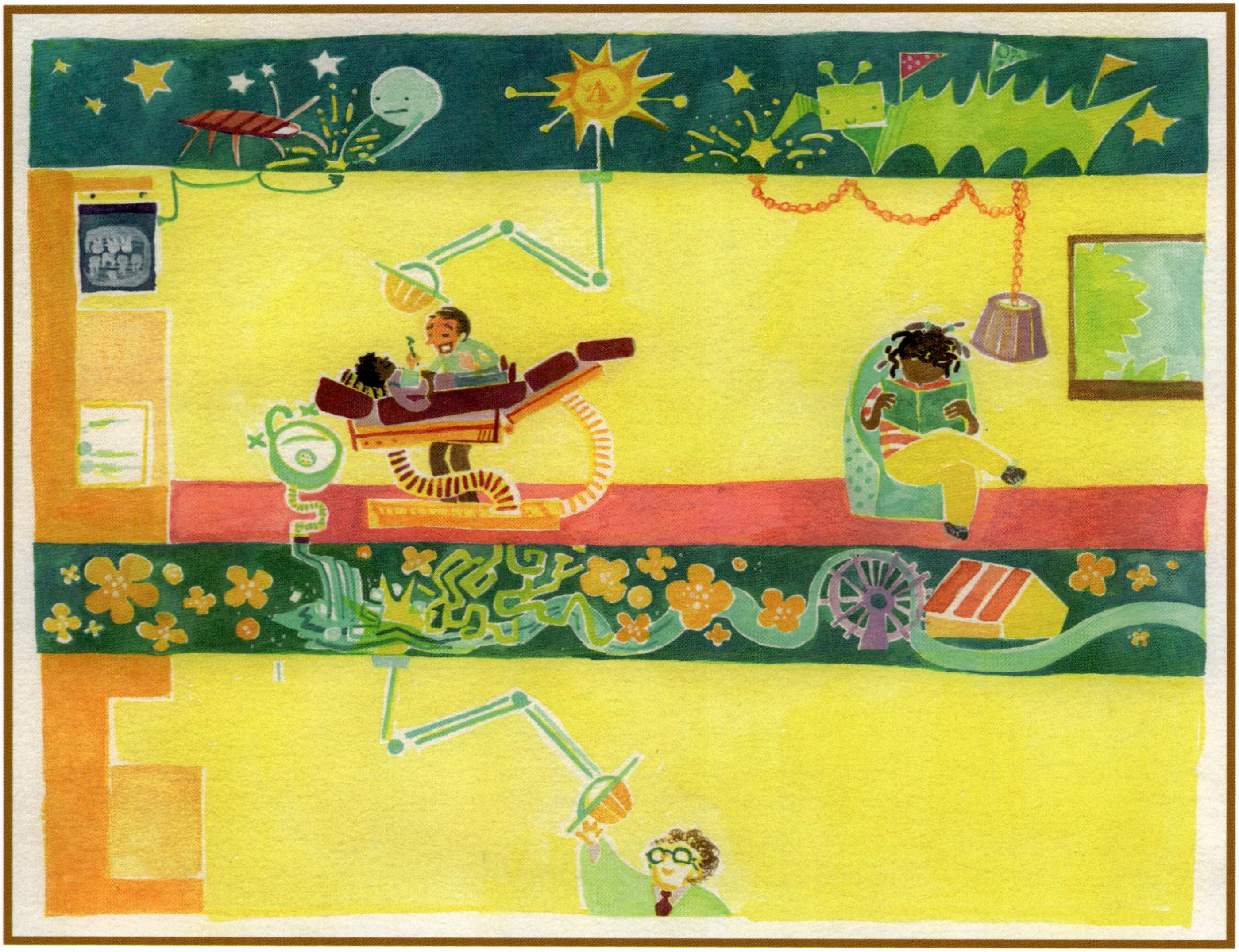

Interstitial Space

In architecture, **Interstitial Space** describes "an accessible space above the ceiling plane with a floor for access and a low vertical height to accomplish a horizontal distribution of systems."[1] Interstitial space is the unseen space that allows places to function.

Interstitial space is a part of the modern built environment. HVAC, plumbing, electricity and other functional elements reside out of sight in these spaces, yet are essential for building function. Interstitial space allows for easy access to essential equipment by service personnel. Though interstitial spaces are essential to the function of everyday places where we work and live, they mostly go unnoticed unless there is a problem. Only when a building is built, or is in need of maintenance, are these interstitial spaces opened and used.

The Internet is filled with interstitial spaces. The general experience of the web has nothing to do with where the information is actually stored. The idea of interstitial space contributes to the almost magical nature of the Internet. The place where emails go after they are sent and before they are read is an example of interstitial space. Though interstitial spaces are seldom seen, these spaces allow the Internet to function.

The marketing-based jargon term 'cloud computing' refers to networked data is stored on hard drives in server racks in remote data centers. Though many people are familiar with jargon term "the cloud," many have no idea how the interstitial spaces of the Internet function, or where their email goes when it is sent.[2] Just like the interstitial space of architecture, these information-based interstitial spaces are only noticeable when there is a problem with the network.

References

1. Cooper, E. Crawley. (1994) *Laboratory Design Handbook.* Boca Raton, FL: CRC Press, 1994; and Ruys, T., AIA. (1990). *Handbook of Facilities Planning, Vol. One, Laboratory Facilities.* Ruys, Theodorus, AIA, (Ed.) New York: Van Nostrand Reinhold.

2. (August 2012) Partly Cloudy – About Cloud Computing. Survey: Many Believe "The Cloud" Requires a Rain Coat. Citrix Cloud Survey Guide. *Wakefield Research.* Retrieved Feb 2, 2013, from http://www.citrix.com/site/resources/dynamic/additional/Citrix-Cloud-Survey-Guide.pdf

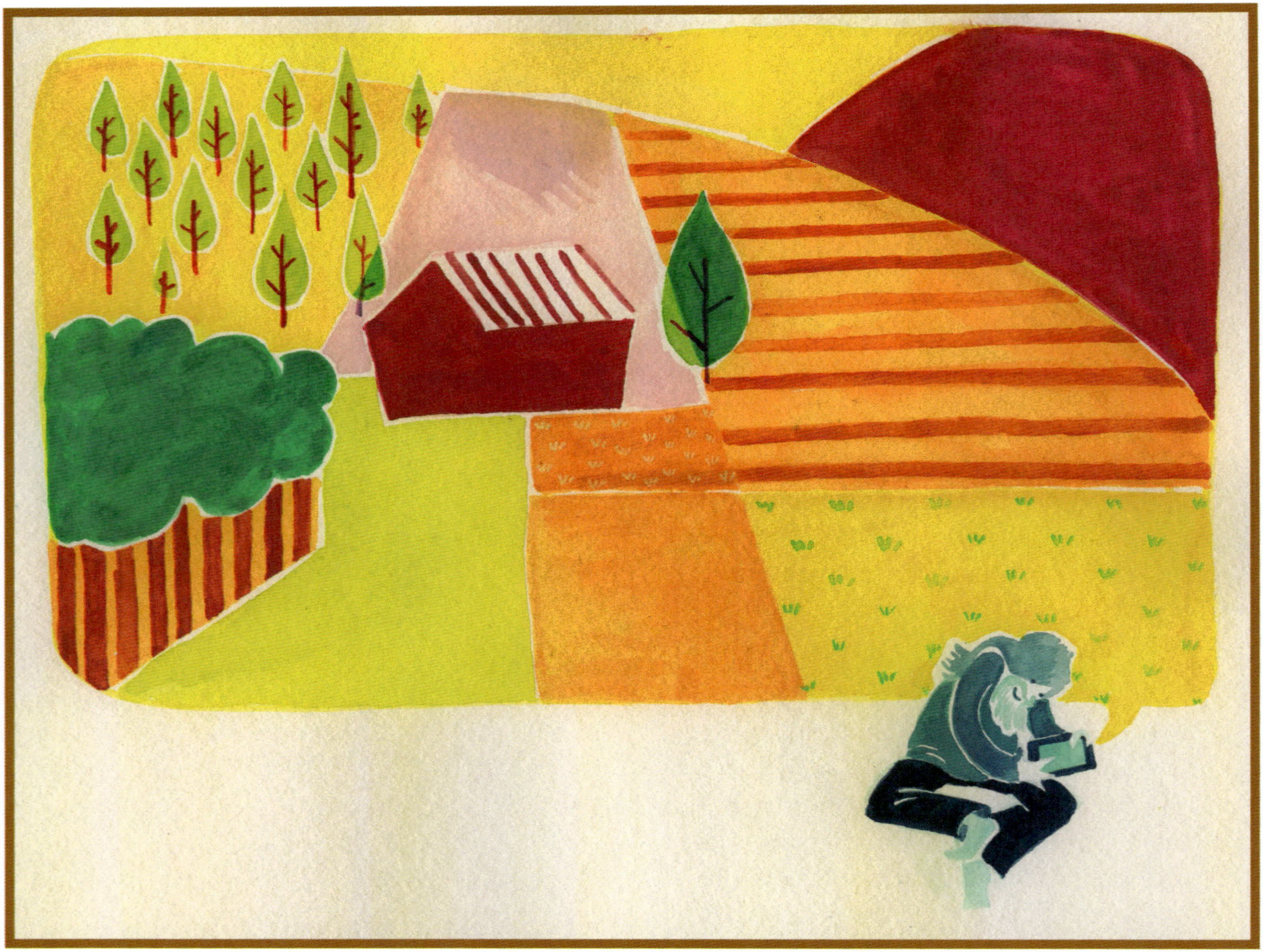

Invisible Space

Invisible Space is a way of describing the new geography created by software running in networked environments. In 2002, Nigel Thrift and Shaun French wrote how the geography of technologically connected societies have changed "as software has come to intervene in nearly all aspects of everyday life."[1]

When one puts an item into a physical bag, it gets heavier. When one puts an item into virtual space, the computer that holds it stays the same weight. Every time a page is accessed it's reproduced for that current user, with little energy required for the replication. Space is easily produced in virtual reality. Virtual space is created with every click on the web, every document uploaded to the web, and every social networking profile. Each of these formats have no physical limitation on space, as there is "in real life."

Related Reading

"Digital Hoarding" on page 37

References

1. Thrift, Nigel and Shaun French. (2002) *The Automatic Production of Space.* University of Bristol: School of Geographical Sciences. Pg. 309.

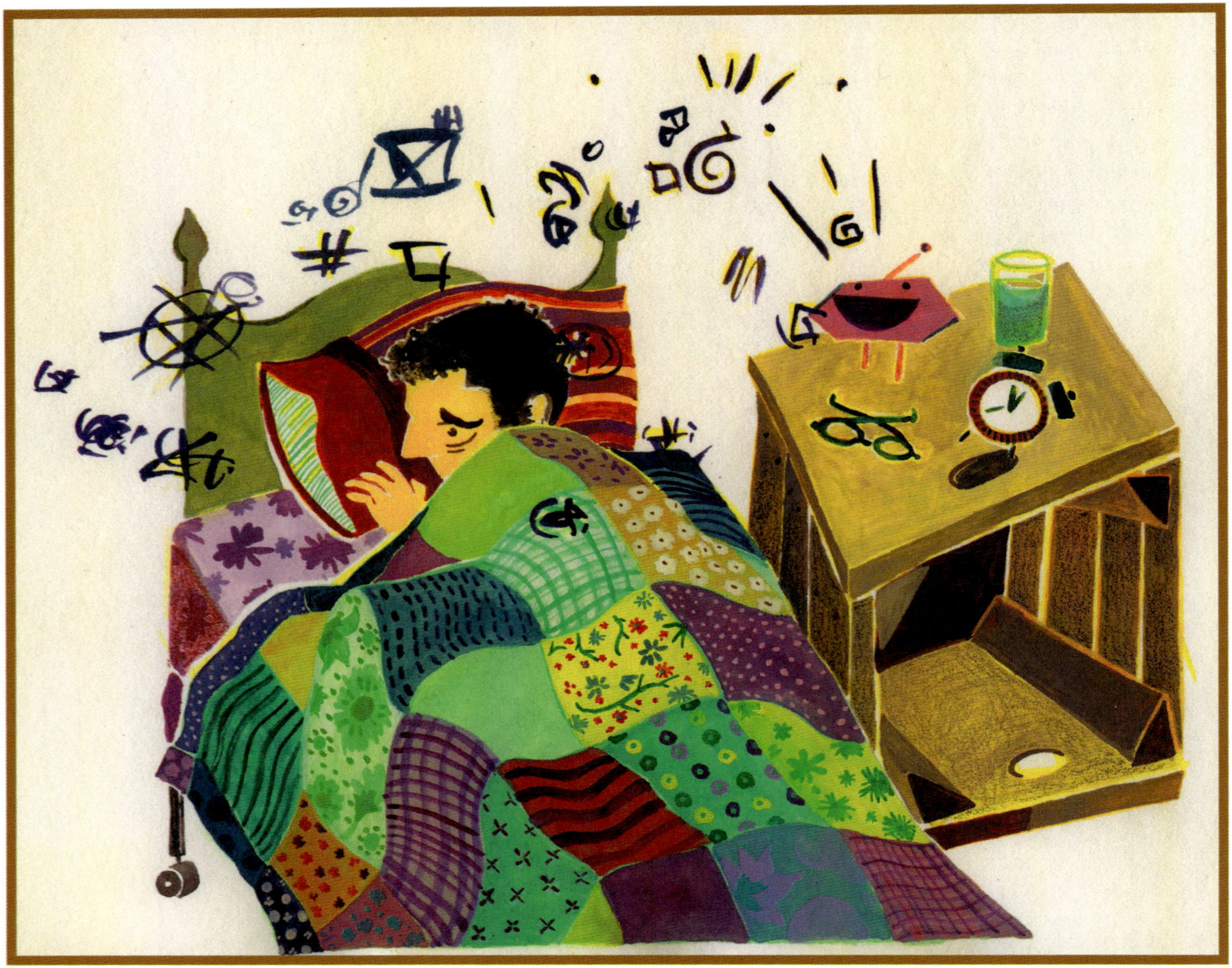

Junk Sleep

Junk sleep was popularized by a group of four undergraduate students at NTU's Wee Kim Wee School of Communication and Information in Singapore.[1] The students hypothesized that the use of electronic devices right before bed might affect sleep in a negative way. They created an educational site called "Good in Bed" about the issues surrounding what they called "Junk Sleep."

In order to avoid Junk Sleep, the students suggested not touching cell phones or laptops at least a half hour before bed. The students mentioned that junk sleep was a result of both the devices and the content displayed on the screens. Both the brightness of the screen and the nature of the content on the device play a role in disrupting the body's natural process of falling asleep.

Several studies such as have been done on the use of electronics and effects on sleep, such as the National Sleep Foundation Poll on technology use and sleep,[2] electronic media use and sleep in adolescents[3] and the effects of backlit screens on melatonin production.[4] Researchers at the Rensselaer Polytechnic Institute found that using a self-luminous device such as a tablet, phone or computer before bed tricks the brain into becoming more active instead of preparing for sleep, leading to a false sense of alertness and a decrease in melatonin production,[5] the chemical naturally produced in the brain before sleep begins. The nature of information on the web can also contribute to increased media time. Unlike the slowly-unfolding narratives of books, social networking and news sites are formatted for quick information consumption. The constant flow of unrelated information can trigger information binges, resulting in more screen time before bed.

References

1. (November 2009) The Big Bedroom Bustup @ Zouk – Overcoming Junk Sleep. *Nanyang Technological University*. Retrieved July 3, 2011, from http://www.wkwsci.ntu.edu.sg/NewsMedia/Pages/NewsReleasesArchival.aspx

2. National Sleep Foundation. (2011) Annual Sleep in America Poll Exploring Connections with Communications Technology Use and Sleep. [Press release]. Retrieved February 13, 2013, from http://www.sleepfoundation.org/article/press-release/annual-sleep-america-poll-exploring-connections-communications-technology-use-

3. Cain, Neralie; Michael Gradisar (2010) Electronic media use and sleep in school-aged children and adolescents: a review. In S. Chokroverty (Ed.) *Sleep Medicine* (pp. 735–742).

4-5. Science Daily (August 2012) Light from Self-Luminous Tablet Computers Can Affect Evening Melatonin, Delaying Sleep. [Press Release] Retrieved February 13, 2013, from http://www.sciencedaily.com/releases/2012/08/120827094211.htm

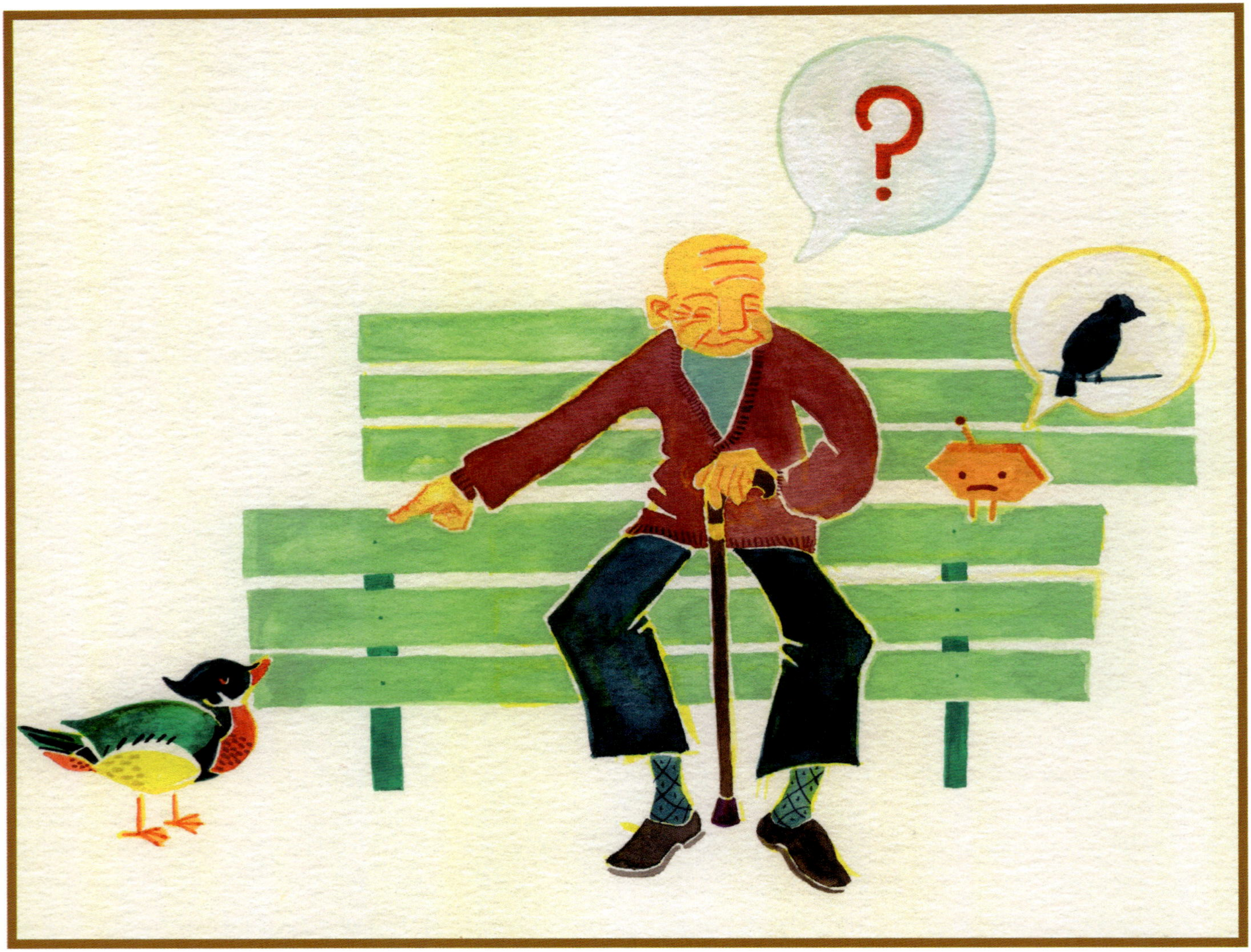

Machine Learning

Machine Learning is a process of training a computer algorithm to properly classify future inputs after having trained the algorithm with sample data. A program is first trained with known inputs, and "learns" the patterns through one or more statistical methods. The program then classifies new input based on the input seen before. Machine Learning is used for many applications, including computer vision, a method used by computers to identify images.[1]

Ray Solomonoff published the first report on non-semantic machine learning in 1956, titled *An Inductive Inference Machine*.[2] Solomonoff was a pioneer in algorithmic probability, publishing several papers on the subject in the 1960s. It wasn't until the late 1970s that machine learning started emerging as a more focused field of study in computer vision.

An example of a machine learning system is a program that can be trained to recognize whether a person is present in images from a security camera feed. The program would first be trained on several known images without a person present in the frame as the negative input, followed by several images with a person in the frame as the positive input. The program would then be able to determine whether a person is present in future images with reasonable accuracy.

Machine learning can be applied to many fields including natural language processing, speech and handwriting recognition, and sentiment analysis. More recently, machine learning has been applied to create search engine algorithms. Researchers at Cornell University created a search engine prototype, STRIVER, which was able to improve its results over time based on which results the visitor clicked on.[3] Facebook engineers also use machine learning techniques to improve spam detection and deliver relevant articles to users based on previous interactions on the site.[4]

References

1. Ajay Joshi, Anoop Cherian and Ravishankar Shivalingam. (2009) Machine Learning in Computer Vision. *Dept. of Computer Science, University of Minnesota.* Retrieved October 2011, from http://www-users.cs.umn.edu/~cherian/ppt/MachineLearningTut.pdf

2. Solomonoff, R. J. (1956) An Inductive Reference Machine. *Technical Research Group.* Retrieved October 2011, from http://world.std.com/~rjs/indinf56.pdf

3. Mitchell, T. (1997) *Machine Learning.* New York: McGraw Hill. Pg. 2.

4. Alexandrescu, Andrei. (January 29, 2012) 10 Questions with Facebook Research Engineer Andrei Alexandrescu. *Server-Side Magazine.* Retrieved March 2013, from http://www.serversidemagazine.com/news/10-questions-with-facebook-research-engineer-andrei-alexandrescu/

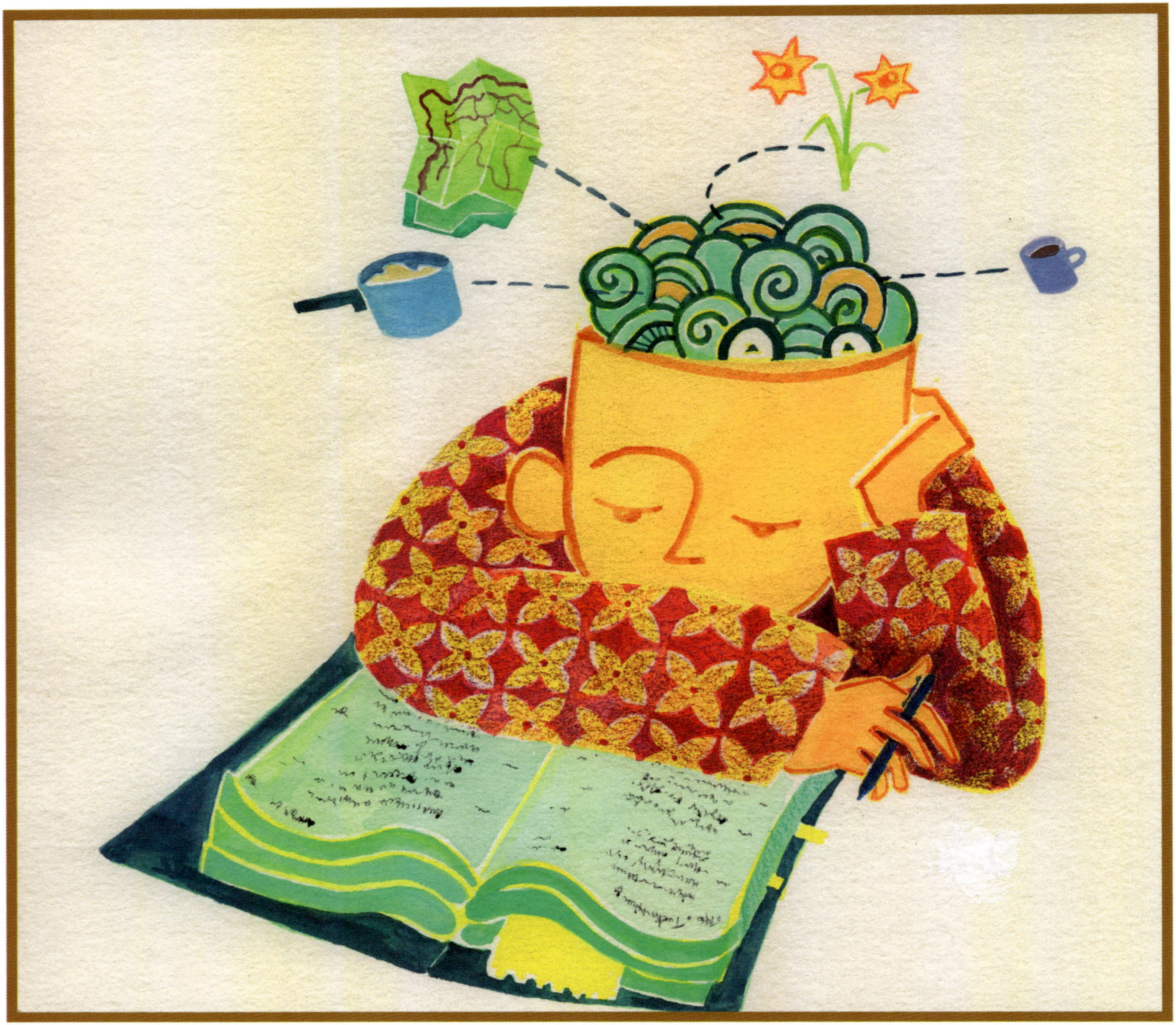

Mental Real Estate

Mental real estate is a way of describing the amount of "space" one has in one's mind, and how much of it is taken up by one idea, brand, or other substance.

A good brand name is memorable through generations. Coca-Cola is affiliated with the moon landing, Christmas and summer, all in one. In 2010, a cross-University study interviewed 38 Australian children ages 3-5 and found that they could correctly speak the brand name affiliated with a given logo, before they could read.[1]

Coca-cola's advertising has significantly affected American Culture, credited with creating the modern image of Santa Claus.[2]

Brands wage wars over mental real estate. The mental real estate that one has when the word "tissue" is mentioned is taken by "Kleenex" but not "Puffs." Mental real estate of consumers is the highest commodity for marketing departments. It is the life or death of a brand. Sometimes, whatever gets into a person's mind first is fixed in place and is very difficult to write over with a later memory. Veteran screenwriter Terry Rossio calls mental real estate the "most valuable real estate in the world."[3]

References

1. McAlister, Anna R. and Cornwell, T. Bettina. (2010) Children's Brand Symbolism Understanding. In Psychology and Marketing. Wiley.

2. Mckay, George. (2008) Consumption, coca-colanisation, cultural resistance--and Santa Claus. In S Whiteley (Ed.) *Christmas, Ideology and Popular Culture.* (Pg 5.) Edinburgh University Press.

3. Rossio, Terry. (2000) Mental Real Estate. *Wordplay.* Retrieved August 3, 2013, from http://wordplayer.com/columns/wp42.Mental.Real.Estate.html

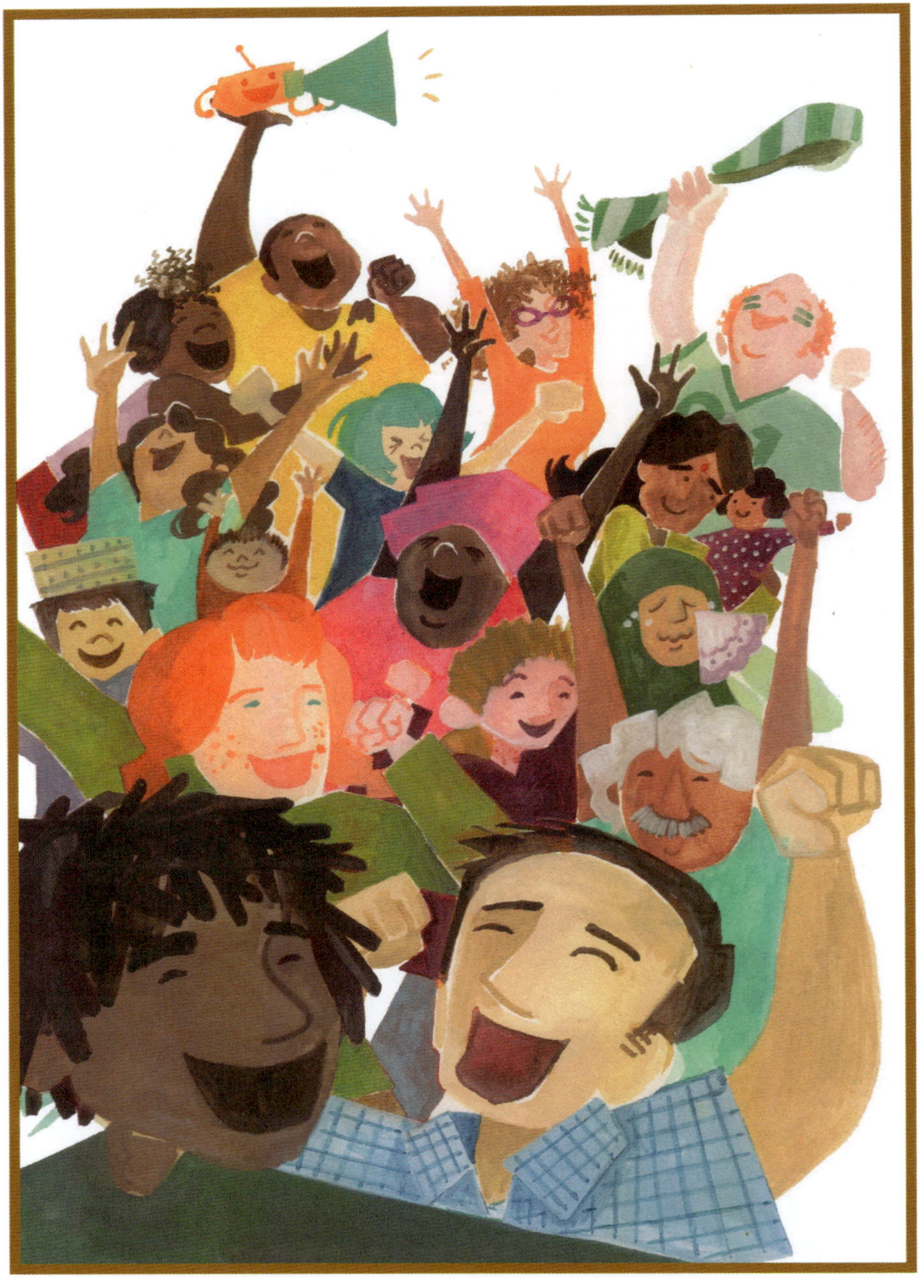

Micro-singularity

A **micro-singularity** describes a moment where everyone connected to a social network or culture experiences a certain moment or thought almost simultaneously.

Though John Von Neuman spoke about the "ever accelerating process of technology" and its eventual convergence in the 1950s, the term singularity was popularized by mathematics professor and science fiction writer Vernor Vinge in 1993.[1]

In a micro-singularity, all media reach a saturation point. Just like a collective consciousness, everyone on an information network has access to the same information at the same time. It's not that everyone is always connected to the same thoughts, but any sufficiently large news story can be quickly pushed through a network so that the entire network is rapidly saturated.

Every large newsworthy event presents a potential micro-singularity. This phenomenon will only increase as more and more people have access to real-time information. Global events bring on temporary micro-singularities in which many communities share the same information at the same time, regardless of topic interest. Earthquakes in China, Haiti and Japan, the World Cup and musician Michael Jackson's death are examples of micro-singularities. Fans of Apple products learn about new releases in a manner that most closely resembles a collective consciousness. The Internet reported a slow-down when Jackson's death was announced.[2]

On May 11th, 2008, a earthquake that measured 7.8 on the Richter scale hit China. Several of those who experienced the earthquake were Twitter users, including @dtan. When @dtan reported the earthquake, Tech Reporter Robert Scoble was able to rebroadcast the message to 40,000 followers.[3] The news traveled more quickly than the earthquake itself.

References

1. Vinge, Vernor. (1993) The Coming Technological Singularity: How to Survive in the Post-Human Era. Retrieved August 2013, from http://www-rohan.sdsu.edu/faculty/vinge/misc/singularity.html

2. Shiels, Maggie. (June 26, 2009) Web slows after Jackson's death. *BBC News.* Retrieved July 2013, from http://news.bbc.co.uk/2/hi/technology/8120324.stm

3. Scoble, Robert. (May 11, 2008) "@dtan just reported an earthquake in Beijing. Wonder how large it is? Off to check out USGS site." Tweet. Retrieved July 2010, from http://twitter.com/Scobleizer/status/809121152

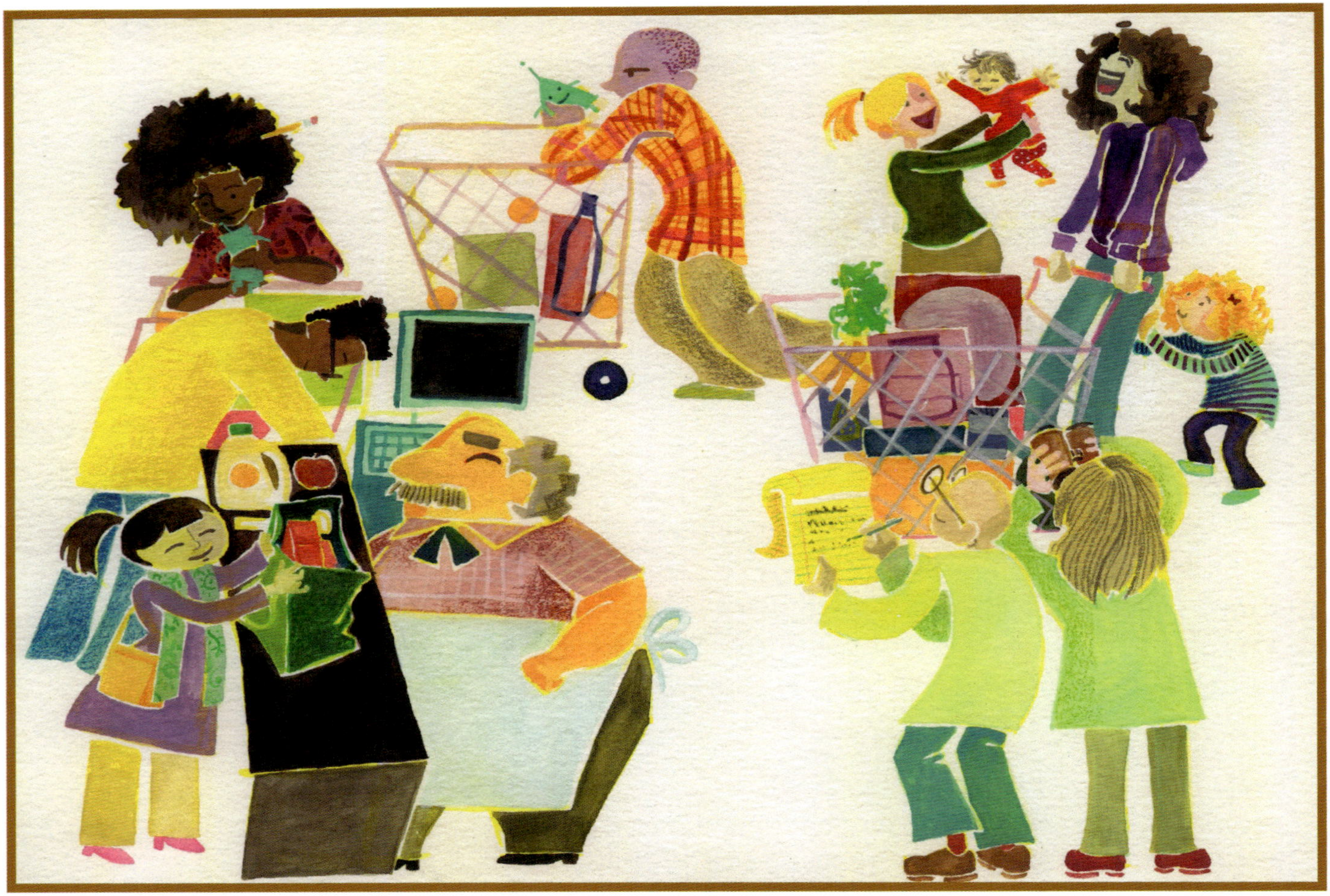

Mundane Studies

Mundane Studies is a term used to describe the study of the events and systems that comprise the experiences of everyday life. Studying everyday life is important in changing societies, especially ones that have been defined and re-created constantly by technology. It is only by studying the everyday that one can understand how much things have changed from one year to the next.

In 2000, sociologist Wayne Brekhus published "A Mundane Manifesto," in which he called for "analytically interesting studies of the socially uninteresting." Brekhus argued that the extraordinary drew "disproportionate theoretical attention from researchers," and that it ultimately hindered the real picture of "social reality." His manifesto sought to pave a way for an "explicit social science of the unmarked (mundane)."[1] Brekhus suggested that while there were many deviance journals to "explicitly analyze socially unusual behavior" there was no "Journal of Mundane Behavior to explicitly analyze conformity."[2]

The mundane relates to how technology is taken for granted and how this affects the way we interact with technology on a day-to-day basis. In the 1870s the landline telephone usage caused concern, supernatural fear and uneasiness for the public at large. These reactions diminished as telephone usage became a social norm.[3] Technology adoption was still slow, causing the telephone to take "five decades to reach 10% of the households in America, while the Web took only five years to reach the same level."[4]

Because we've slowly become accustomed to mobile phones and small glass screens, it is no longer a big deal to see commuters on a bus or train stare into small screens for hours at a time in 2013, a behavior that would seem entirely bizarre only 10 years ago in 2003.

References

1. Brekhus, Wayne. (2000) Mundane Manifesto. *Journal of Mundane Behavior.* Retrieved July 2013, from http://www.mundanebehavior.org/issues/v1n1/brekhus.htm

2. Calvin, Rich. (2009) Mundane SF 101. In K. Hellekson (Ed.) *SFRA Review 289 (Summer 2009)* (pp. 13–16). Retrieved October 2010, from http://www.sfra.org/sfra-review/289.pdf

3. Brooks, J. (1975) *Telephone: The First Hundred Years.* New York: Harper & Row.

4. Fischer, C. S. (1992) *America calling: A social history of the telephone to 1940.* Berkeley: University of California Press.

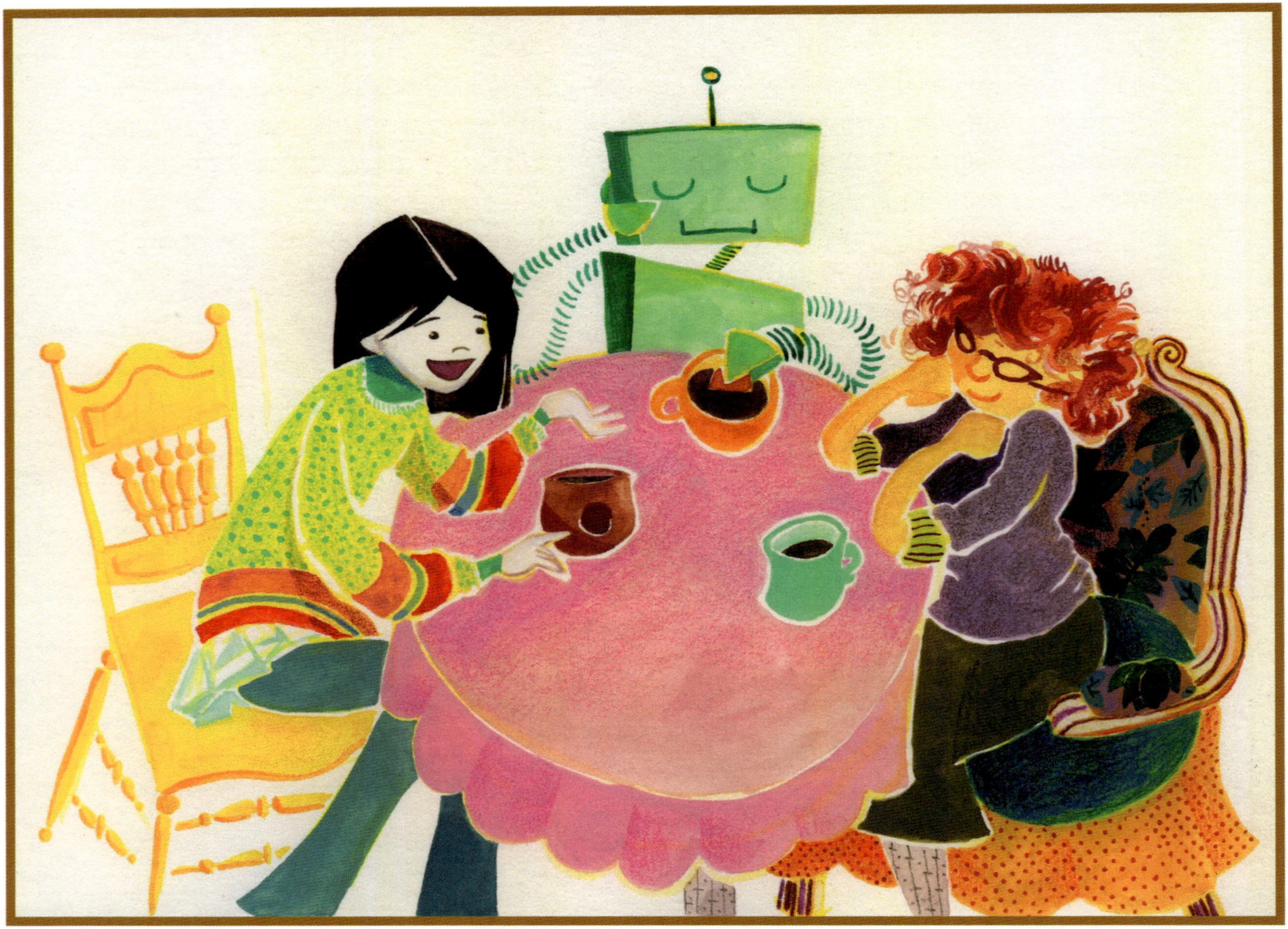

Natural Language Processing

Natural Language Processing, or NLP, is a field of computer science that deals with text from human languages, both spoken and written. A common NLP task is translating spoken words to written text, and a relatively well-solved problem is part-of-speech tagging, where a computer can correctly identify the parts of speech of each word in a sentence.

The goal of NLP is to accomplish human-like language processing. The choice of the word "processing" is very deliberate, and should not be replaced with "understanding," as a computer can only process and correlate information, while only a human can understand.[1]

Although the field of NLP was originally referred to as Natural Language Understanding (NLU) in the early days of AI, it is well agreed today that while the goal of NLP is true NLU, that goal has not yet been accomplished. A full NLU System would be able to paraphrase an input text, translate the text into another language, answer questions about the contents of the text, and draw inferences.

While NLP has made serious inroads into accomplishing goals 1 to 3, despite the fact that NLP systems cannot, of themselves, draw inferences from text, NLU still remains the goal of NLP.[2] There are many other applications of natural language processing, including producing a summary of a block of text, optical character recognition, handwriting recognition, sentiment analysis, and machine translation.

Siri and Google Now are examples of systems that use NLP to interpret human requests. There have been some limitations of these systems, namely the inability for Siri to interpret people with heavy accents, or slang terms.[3]

References

1-2. Xiaoyong Liu. (January 27, 2009) Natural Language Processing. *Center for Natural Language Processing.* Retrieved October 2011, from http://www.cnlp.org/publications/03nlp.lis.encyclopedia.pdf

3. Pinchefsky, Carol. (February 1, 2013) Siri Fails to Understand Scottish Accent in Hilarious Video. *Forbes.* Retrieved May 2013, from http://www.forbes.com/sites/carolpinchefsky/2012/02/01/siri-fails-to-understand-scottish-accent-in-hilarious-video/

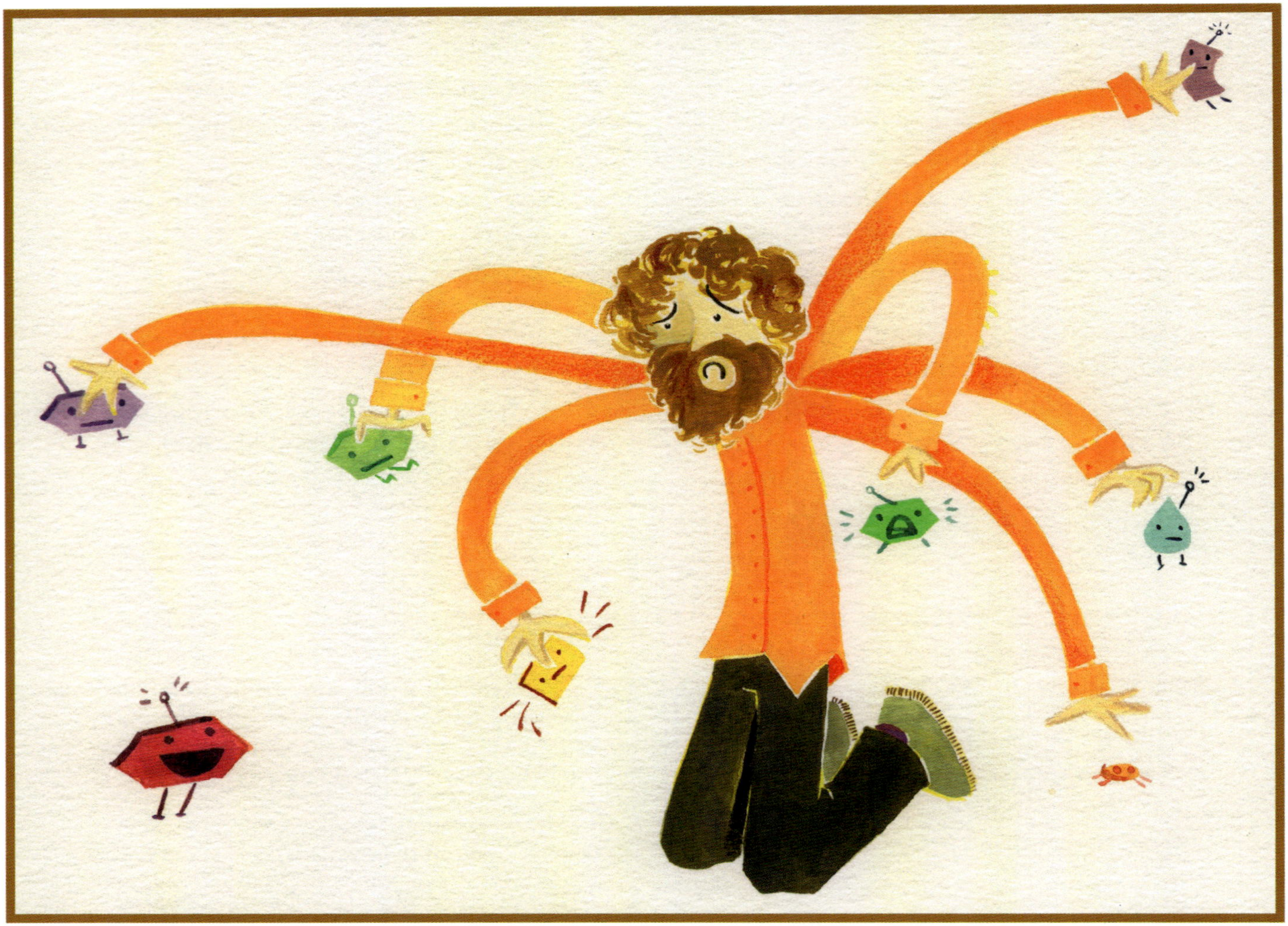

Panic Architecture

Panic architecture is a term used to describe a participatory architecture that demands compulsive interaction or attention.

Email accounts list many items at once that require a response. Tech writer Leisa Reichelt discovered that simply looking at emails throw users into a kind of panic or state of suspended breathing. She coined the term "Email Apnea" to describe the unconscious process of holding one's breath checking email.[1]

B.F. Skinner's experiments on behaviorism found that rats who got irregular food rewards from pushing a lever were far more driven to compulsively push the bar in hopes of receiving a reward.[2] Skinner called this compulsive behavior intermittent reinforcement. The intermittent nature of emails and social networks invite people to obsessively check to see if new email or content is there.[3] Linda Stone's solution is what she calls "conscious computing,"[4] a series of systems to remind the self to take breaks, breathe, and consider the computer as a tool.

Email and social networks are just a few examples of systems that inspire panic and dedication. One early example of a panic architecture is the Tamogotchi pocket pet, an electronic virtual pet encased in a plastic egg shape. The Tamogotchi pocket pet prodded users into caring for a virtual creature at rapid intervals. The Tamogotchi-like nature of virtual farming game Farmville entangling users into "a web of social obligations"[5] in a similar way by exposing 'needs' of virtual items such as crops and animals, causing dedicated users to "care for" these systems on set intervals. This tangled web of social obligations increased in-game time and kept users coming back to the site. At its most extreme, this kind of reward structure can lead to 'binge gaming' where users play for hours or days at a time, often to death.[6]

References

1. Stone, Linda. (November 30, 2007) Diagnosis: Email Apnea. *Lindastone.net*. Retrieved March 31, 2013, from http://lindastone.net/2009/11/30/diagnosis-email-apnea/

2. Webb, Matt, and Tom Stafford. (September 2006) Why email is Addictive and What to do About it. *Mindhacks*. Retrieved October 2011, from http://mindhacks.com/2006/09/19/why-email-is-addictive-and-what-to-do-about-it/

3. Snyder, Daniel. (September 1, 2010) Intermittent Reinforcement: Are You Addicted to email and Smartphones? *Factoidz.com*. Retrieved October 2011, from http://factoidz.com/intermittent-reinforcement-are-you-addicted-to-email-and-smartphones/

4. Stone, Linda. (April 20, 2012) Conscious Computing. *Lindastone.net*. Retrieved March 31, 2013, from http://lindastone.net/2012/04/20/conscious-computing-36/

5. Liszkiewicz, Patrick A. J. (March 09, 2010) Cultivated Play: Farmville. *Mediacommons*. Accessed March 31, 2013, from http://mediacommons.futureofthebook.org/content/cultivated-play-farmville

6. Huffington Post. (July 2012) Diablo 3 Death: Teen Dies After Playing Game For 40 Hours Straight. Retrieved July 2013, from http://www.huffingtonpost.com/2012/07/18/diablo-3-death-chuang-taiwan-_n_1683036.html

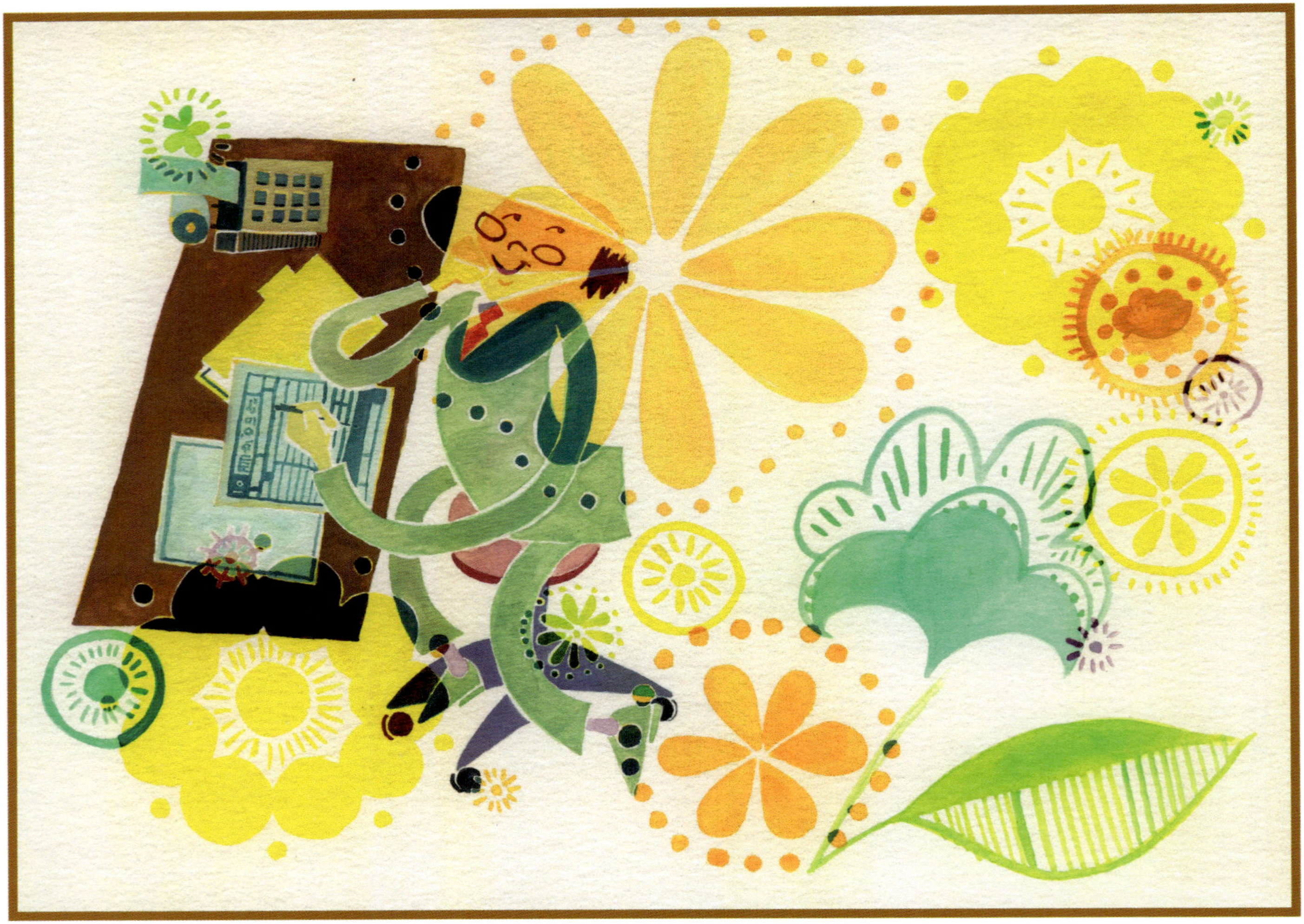

Paracosmic Immersion

Paracosm is a term used to describe the phenomenon of an imaginary friend, "an elaborated private society or even an alternative world."[1] The concept of a paracosm was first described by a researcher for the BBC, Robert Silvey, with later research by British psychiatrist Stephen A. MacKeith, and British psychologist David Cohen.[2]

Paracosms are often mentioned in articles on childhood creativity and problem-solving. Some scholars believe paracosm play indicates high intelligence. A Michigan State University study revealed that many MacArthur Fellows Program recipients had paracosms as children.[3]

The period between 9-10 years old, when kids have the most paracosmic activity, is incredibly important in a child's life,[4] says open data advocate Max Ogden. Research has shown that many adults with high levels of paracosmic activity in childhood grow up to participate more readily in the creative economy.[5] To the interface designer, adds Ogden, building wireframes is related to paracosmic immersion. Properly designing an interface requires a designer to try on different personas, invent different types of users, and see through their eyes. It requires critical thinking, analysis, imagination and creativity, anticipating how a certain user or group of users might approach design problems. Synthesizing these variables together is a process helped by those who are good at imagining alternate realities.[6]

"The moral of the story is this," Ogden concludes, "if you have a 9-10 year old, make sure they have imaginary friends, or they will have boring desk jobs for the rest of their lives."[7]

References

1. Singer, Dorothy G., Singer, Jerome L., (1992) *The House of Make-Believe: Children's Play and the Developing Imagination.* Cambridge: Harvard University Press.

2. Cohen, David and MacKeith, Stephen. (1992) *The Development of Imagination: The Private Worlds of Childhood.* London: Routledge.

3. Taylor, Marjorie. (2001) *Imaginary Companions and the Children Who Create Them.* Oxford University Press.

4-7. Interview with software developer Max Ogden in Portland, Oregon. July 31, 2010.

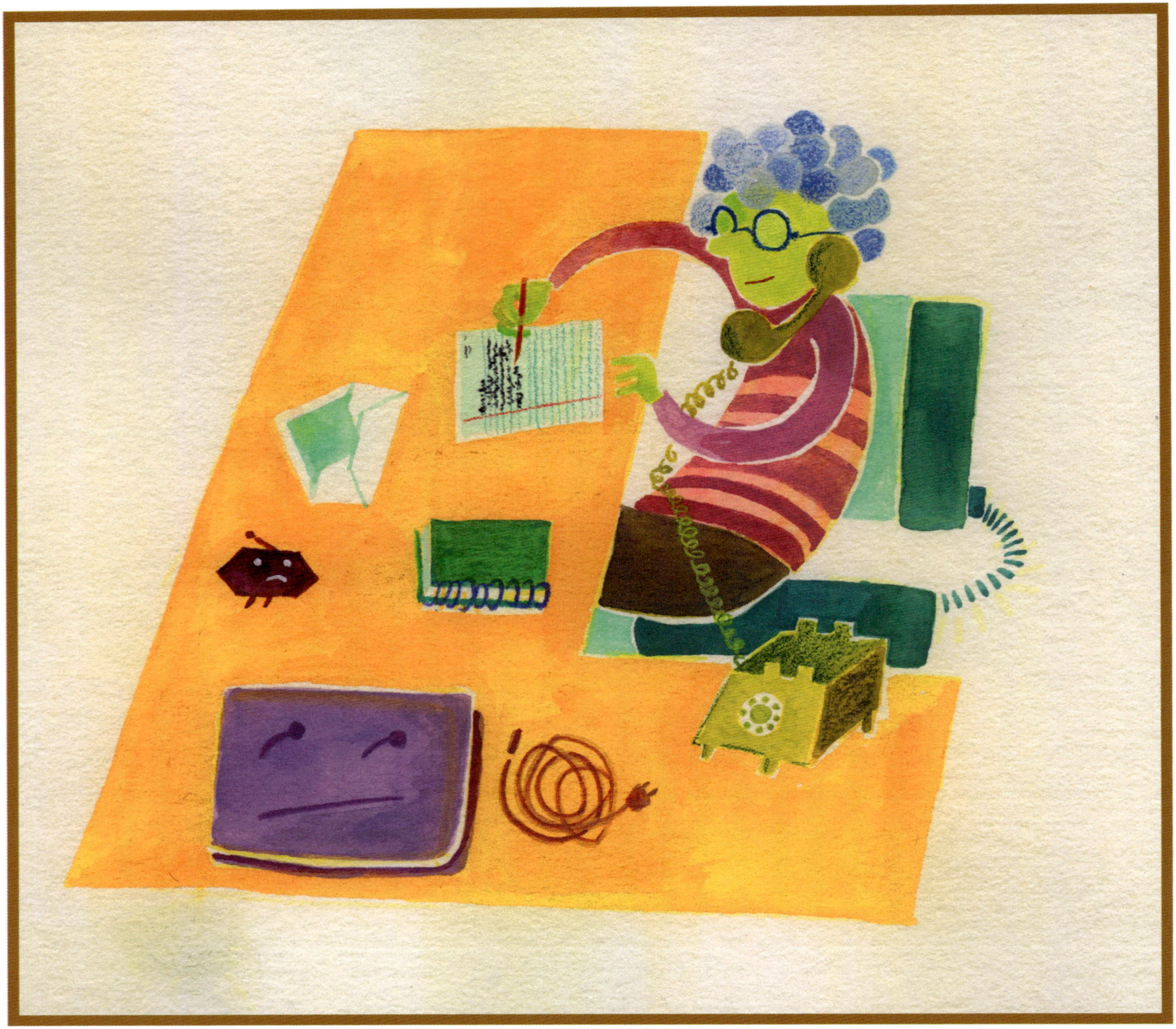

Path Dependence

Path dependence is a term used to describe the tendency of individuals to use the same systems over time instead of adopting new ones. Path dependence describes a person's behavior and reluctance to change it, even when offered a more efficient alternative. Though more efficient input devices may exist, the tendency for the general public to stick with the same devices over decades of technological change and development blocks the adoption of alternative technologies.

Once an individual, group or culture becomes accustomed to doing things one way, it is difficult to start over and start doing things another way. Someone who uses a landline phone and writes letters as primary forms of communication instead of adopting new methods is an example of someone with path dependence. Though cell phones and text messages may be more efficient forms of communication, the individual's path dependence makes it difficult to transition to these new and unfamiliar methods. In many cases, it takes an external change with large enough magnitude to get an individual to change their behavior. If an individual's social group uses to using cell phones and text messages, the individual may be more likely to make a transition. Path dependence describes why most keyboards still come with QWERTY layouts instead of a more efficient arrangement of frequently-used keys. The "QWERTY keyboard was designed to slow down typing to avoid mechanical typewriter hammers from jamming," we still use it today.[1]

The most popular alternative to QWERTY is DVORAK, a key-arrangement designed to minimize finger movement while typing. Frequently-used keys are placed in positions that are easiest to reach. DVORAK keyboards allow for sustained typing speeds of up to 170 WPM, as achieved by Barbara Blackburn of Salem, Oregon in 1985.[2] Despite this, the uptake of DVORAK has always been slow, as QWERTY is the most prevalent starter method for typing education.[3]

Some pieces of software or hardware persist simply because they were introduced to a large number of people with their first experience with a computer. Though a mouse does not provide the best method of data input, alternative devices such as chorded keyboards did not achieve enough distribution and uptake to replace the mouse.

References

1,3. David, Paul A. (May 1985) Clio and the Economics of QWERTY. *The American Economic Review, Vol. 75, No. 2, Papers and Proceedings of the Ninety-Seventh Annual Meeting of the American Economic Association.* (pp. 332-337).

2. Barbara Blackburn, the World's Fastest Typist. Retrieved August 19, 2013, from http://rcranger.mysite.syr.edu/famhist/blackburn.htm

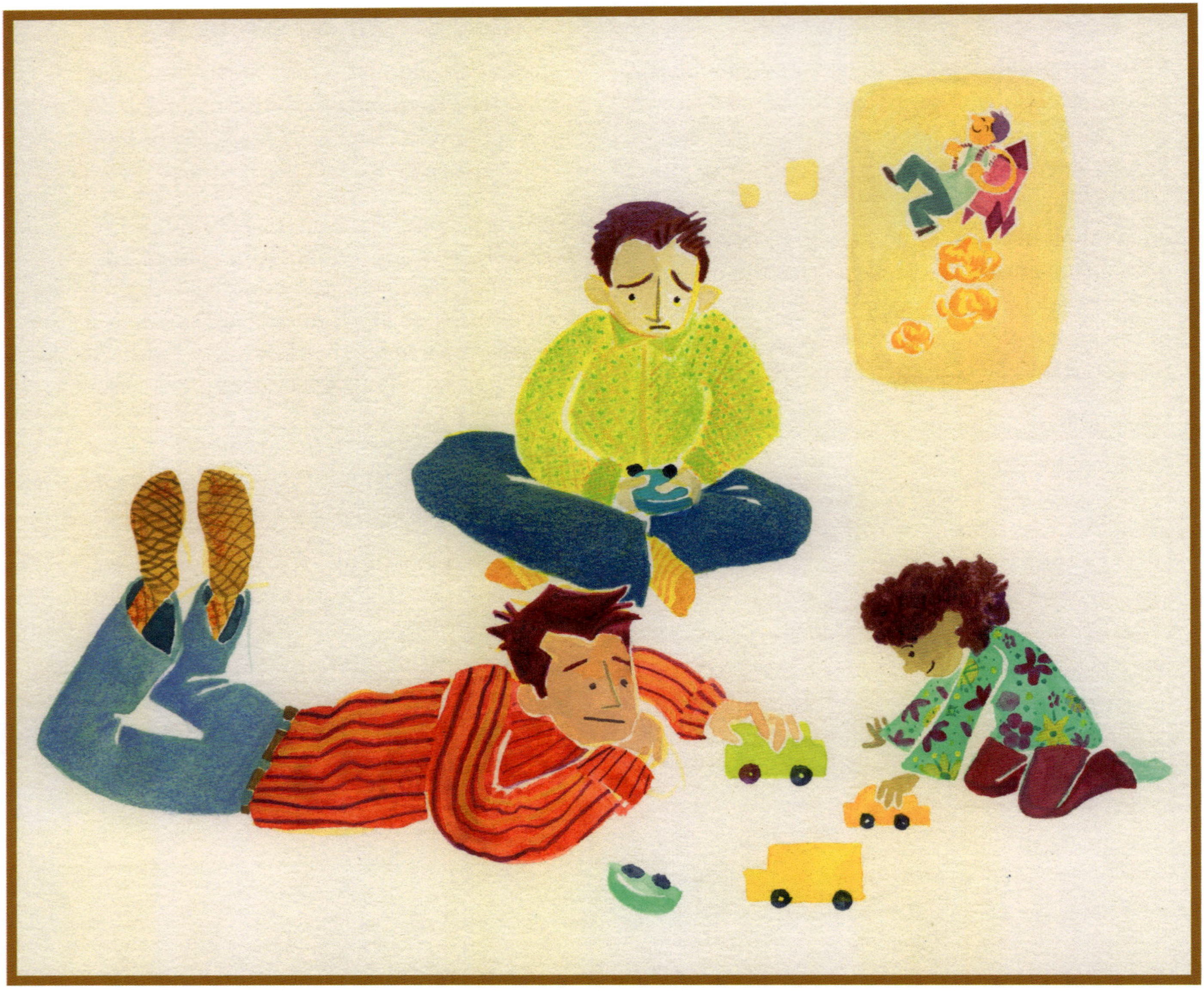

Persistent Architecture

Standard-issue computer mice and keyboards are examples of **persistent architecture**. Unlike path dependence, which is behavior-driven, persistent architecture is about market-driven development, and the tendency for markets to stagnate around working technologies instead of shift to better ones.

Mouse inventor Doug Englebart did not expect the mouse to be a permanent or long-lasting solution to data manipulation and input but rather a step toward a better input device, or direct input such as the touch screen.[1] Instead, the computer mouse persisted and later proliferated into the mass computer market, becoming a mainstay on desks in home and professional computing environments.

With the exception of a few systems like as POS (point of sale) touch screens, the mouse stuck as the default user interface for decades. Apple computer's touch devices were the first challenge to a long period of architectural stagnation.[2] It wasn't until Apple released touchscreen products and the "magic trackpad" in the early 2000s that the computer mouse began to lose its dominant hold on the general public. Once an alternative input method such as the touchscreen was sufficiently developed, the general public found it very easy to change behavior and adopt many mobile devices with touchscreens instead of a mouse. Competitors followed suit, and touchscreen-based products soared in production and adoption.

Some persistent architectures provide a standard with which many people can communicate over time without worrying about compatibility. PDFs and Powerpoint files can be read by the most popular operating systems, and web browsers allow us to view most websites, regardless of programming language the website was written in.

References

1. Derouchey, Bill. (January 11, 2007) iPhone: Future of the Button. *Push Click Touch.* Retrieved April 1, 2013, from http://www.pushclicktouch.com/blog/?p=89

2. Author Unknown. (December 5, 2009) Douglas Engelbart. *I, Programmer.* Retrieved July 2, 2011, from http://www.i-programmer.info/history/people/497-doug-engelbart.html

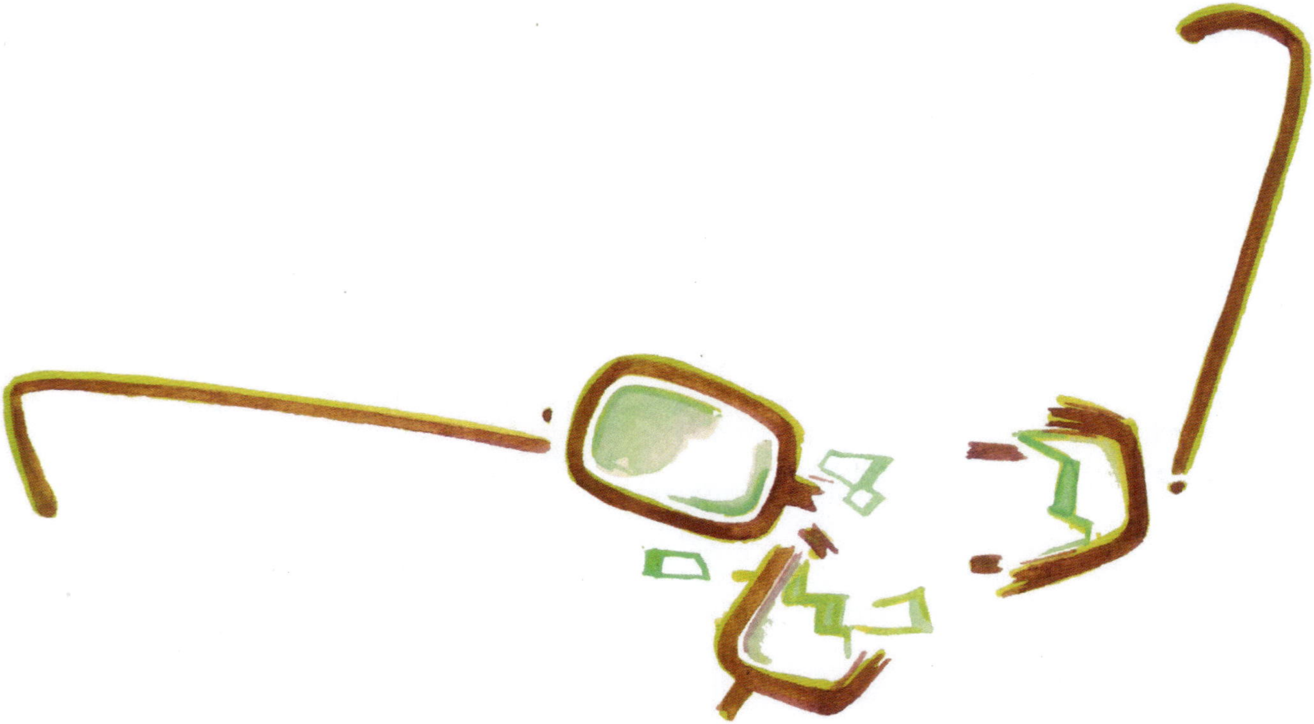

Prosthetics

The word **Prosthetic** describes any object that is a replacement or addition to the body. The term prosthetic comes from the ancient greek word prósthesis, meaning "addition."[1] We all use some form of prosthetics every day, be it shoes, glasses or smartphones. Some prosthetics are cosmetic, while others are solely functional. Some prosthetics, such as prosthetic legs or cochlear implants, are considered restorative or normalizing, as they bring a user to a societally defined "norm," while other prosthetics enhance our experience of the world above the norm. Phones and computers are mental and sensory prosthetics, and these devices extend our capability to see, hear and understand, and our brain treats our prosthetic devices as part of our bodies.[2]

Drawbacks of Prosthetics

In *Civilization and its Discontents*, Sigmund Freud wrote that man has "become a kind of prosthetic God. When he puts on all his auxiliary organs he is truly magnificent; but those organs have not grown on to him and they still give him much trouble at times."[3] Those without the means to constantly upgrade are forced to deal with outdated software and user experience.

Prosthetics and Empowerment

Double amputee Aimee Mullins has over a dozen pairs of prosthetic legs.[4] One pair is made entirely of clear glass and another of woven carbon-fiber. Her carbon-fiber 'cheetah' legs helped her to set World Records in the 100 meter, the 200 meter, and the long jump.[5] Prosthetics and athletes made headlines in 2012 when South Africa's Oscar Pistorious became the first athlete to compete "using prosthetics running blades in the Olympic Games, simultaneously making history and raising the debate over fairness and equality to a whole new platform."[6]

References

1. Prosthesis. *Merriam-Webster Online Dictionary.* Retrieved February 2, 2013, from http://www.merriam-webster.com/dictionary/prosthesis

2. Science Daily. (March 2013) *Human Brain Treats Prosthetic Devices as Part of the Body.* Retrieved August 2013, from http://www.sciencedaily.com/releases/2013/03/130306221135.htm

3. Freud, Sigmund. (1931) *Civilization and its Discontents.* Vienna: Internationaler Psychoanalytischer Verlag. Pg. 44.

4. Mullins, Aimee. (March 2009) It's not fair having 12 pairs of legs. *TED.* Retrieved Feb 2, 2013, from http://www.ted.com/talks/aimee_mullins_prosthetic_aesthetics.html

5. Mullins used the The Össur, Flex-Foot® Cheetah®. *Aimee Mullins Biography.* Retrieved February 2, 2013, from http://www.aimeemullins.com/about.php

6. Oscar Pistorius. *Össur Orthopaedics Corporate Site.* Retrieved February 2013, from http://www.ossur.com/?PageID=13008

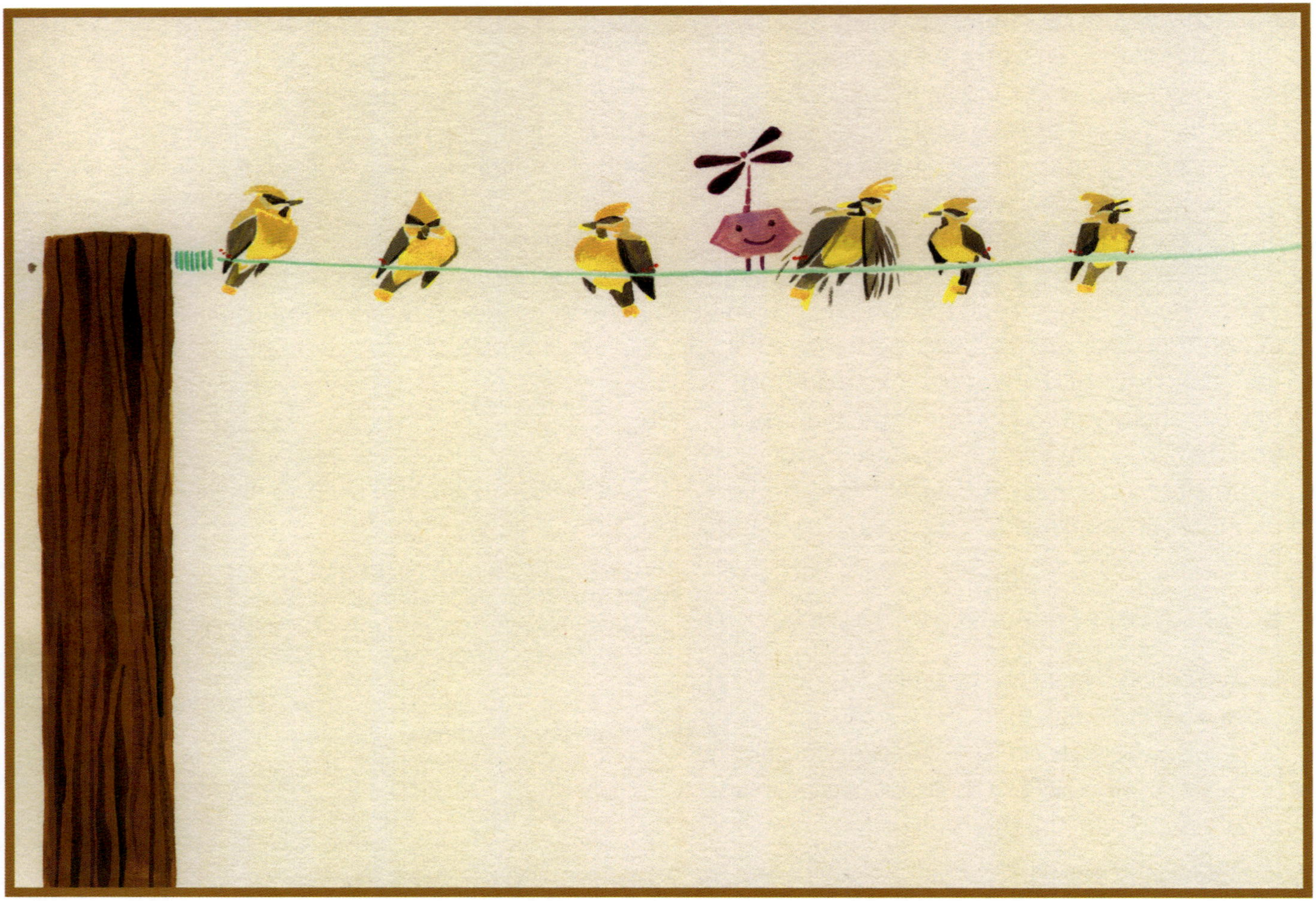

Proxemics

Proxemics describe the space around a person in a given social structure or situation. Proxemics are part of the tacit rules of culture and cultural groups, and are a form of auxiliary communication. Proxemics as a concept was first introduced by Edward T. Hall in his book *The Hidden Dimension*[1] in 1966. "Body spacing and posture," according to Hall, "are unintentional reactions to sensory fluctuations or shifts, such as subtle changes in the sound and pitch of a person's voice. Social distance between people is reliably correlated with physical distance, as are intimate and personal distance..."[2]

Paralanguage

The concept of proxemics is a part of paralanguage. In real life, non-verbal communication such as stance, spatial distance, and non-verbal communications such as gestures and clothing make up paralanguage, contributing to 70% of a culture's communication patterns.[3] Online, paralanguage takes the form of response time and shared information such as pictures, wall posts and other creations of self not expressed in words.

Cultural Differences

Interpersonal space differs from country to country. Morrison and Conaway's report *Global Business Basics* state that in "much of Asia, people gravitate towards other people. For example, if you are alone in an elevator in the Philippines and another person enters, he will probably stand right next to you. That person doesn't want to speak to you; it's just the local custom. If you are sitting in an Indian movie theater surrounded by empty seats and an Indian enters, he is likely to sit next to you."[4] These customs differ greatly from socially acceptable proxemic practices in the mainstream cultures of the United States.

References

1-2. Hall, Edward T. (1966) *The Hidden Dimension*. New York: Anchor Books.

3. Engleberg, Isa N. (2006) Working in Groups: Communication Principles & Strategies. Boston: Houghton Mifflin College. Pg. 133.

4. Morrison, Terri and Conaway, Wayne A. (2000) The Problems of Proxemics. In *Industry Week*. Cleveland: Penton Media.

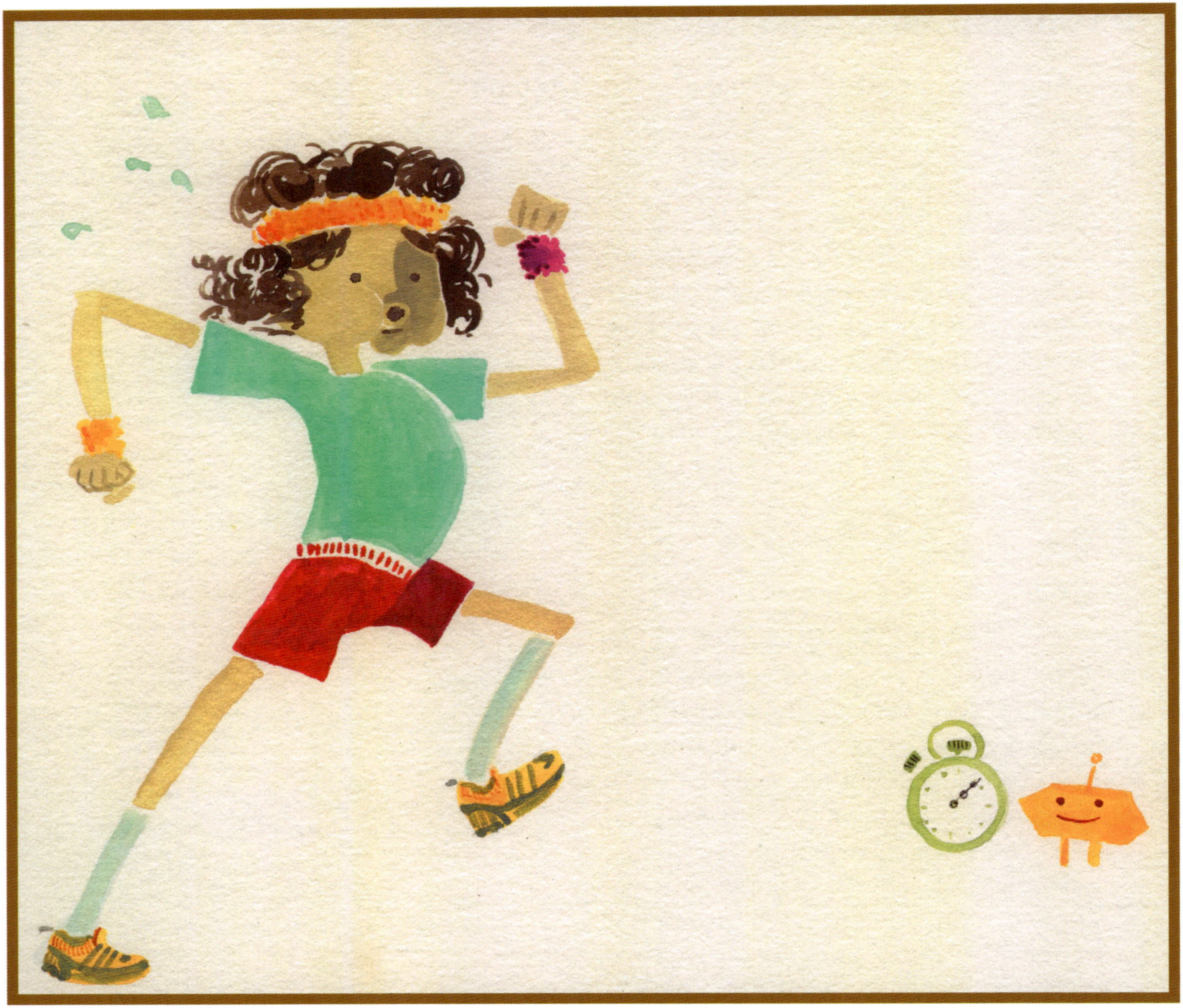

Quantified Self

Quantified self describes the practice of using technology to track statistics and data about one's life in an attempt to visualize and understand more about one's behaviors over time. Quantified self technology allows one to gather data using low-friction methods[1] that are non-invasive or disruptive to everyday life. The advent of low-cost wearable technologies allowed the quantified self movement to proliferate.[2]

The opportunity of the quantified self lies not in the sensors themselves but in the correlation of multiple datasets. Sensors in wearable technology are able to gather speed, time of day, sleep patterns, mood or weight. These statistics are valuable when they are correlated with other datasets, as collected data can provide useful feedback about one's activities over time. Jawbone's *Up Band* tracks steps, sleep and meals, producing "insights" for wearers related to these inputs.[3]

There are two major trends in the quantified self community. Some individuals track for the excitement of gathering data, and are interested in longitudinal data collection. Others track individual data with the express intent to use that data to modify personal behavior. These individuals often use their data as a feedback loop in order to improve their overall health or an aspect of their lives.

The Harvard *Track Your Happiness Project* is one example of short-term survey that examined emotion and external variables over a three month period. Three times a day, participants were prompted by their smartphone to fill out a quick survey of their current happiness level, where they were, who they were with, and what they were doing. Three months later, participants received a series of graphs correlating happiness with this data over time.[4] This information could be used to see behavioral trends not normally accessible on a daily basis.

References

1. Parecki, Aaron. (October 28, 2012) Low Friction Personal Data Collection. Retrieved January 2013, from http://aaronparecki.com/articles/2012/10/28/1/low-friction-personal-data-collection

2. Mann, Steve; Nolan, Jason; Wellman, Barry. (2003) Sousveillance: Inventing and Using Wearable Computing Devices for Data Collection in Surveillance Environments. In *Surveillance & Society* (pp. 1(3): 331-355). Ontario.

3. Jawbone UP FAQ. Retrieved July 2013, from https://jawbone.com/up/faq

5. About Us. *Track Your Happiness.* Retrieved January 2013, from http://www.trackyourhappiness.org/about. To see an example of results from this project, see http://caseorganic.com/wiki/Track_Your_Happiness

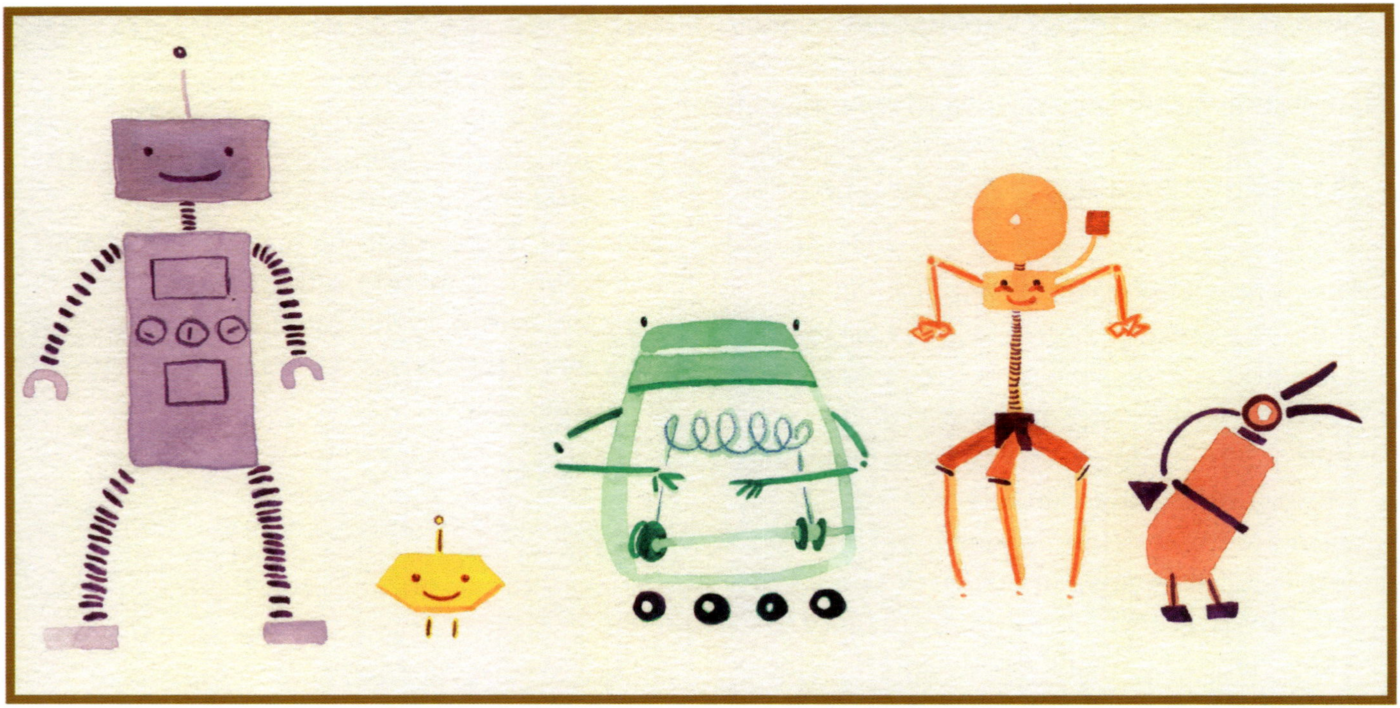

Robot

The word **robot** comes from the 1921 science fiction play "R.U.R." by Karel Čapek[1]. The first robot in literature could be the Tik-Tok, a wind-up mechanical man found by the protagonist in L. Frank Baum's 1907 *Ozma of Oz*, the third book in the famous *Wizard of Oz* series.

Merriam-Webster defines robot as a "machine that looks like a human being and performs various complex acts (as walking or talking) of a human being," a "device that automatically performs complicated often repetitive tasks," or a "mechanism guided by automatic controls."[2] Some robots are made to resemble humans, but the majority of bots are not. Many human-shaped robots, better known as Androids, incite an "uncanny valley"[3], a term originally coined by Masahiro Mori in 1970 to describe the eerie and unsettling response of someone when confronted with an technology that resembles a human but is not quite human.

Humans are surrounded by robots every day, many of them unseen. Google employs "bots" to index webpages and present them to searchers.[4] Unlike the human-shaped image of a robot, search engine bots have no definite shape or form but preform invisible functions for anyone who enters information into a search bar.

The best robots are those that are shaped to perform a single function very well. Unlike Honda's ASIMO, iRobot's Roomba vacuum cleaners are shaped to perform the single task of vacuuming by containing only the features essential to the task instead of trying to replicate an entire human.

References

1. Robot. *Wiktionary.* Retrieved October 2011, from http://en.wiktionary.org/wiki/robot

2. Robot. *Merriam-Webster Dictionary.* Retrieved August 4, 2008, from http://www.merriam-webster.com/dictionary/robot

3. Mori, Masahiro (1970) Bukimi no tani the uncanny valley. Energy, 7, 33–35. (Japanese). Retrieved December 30, 2012 from http://www.androidscience.com/theuncannyvalley/proceedings2005/uncannyvalley.html

4. Googlebot. *Google Webmaster Tools.* Retrieved October 2011, from http://support.google.com/webmasters/bin/answer.py?hl=en&answer=182072

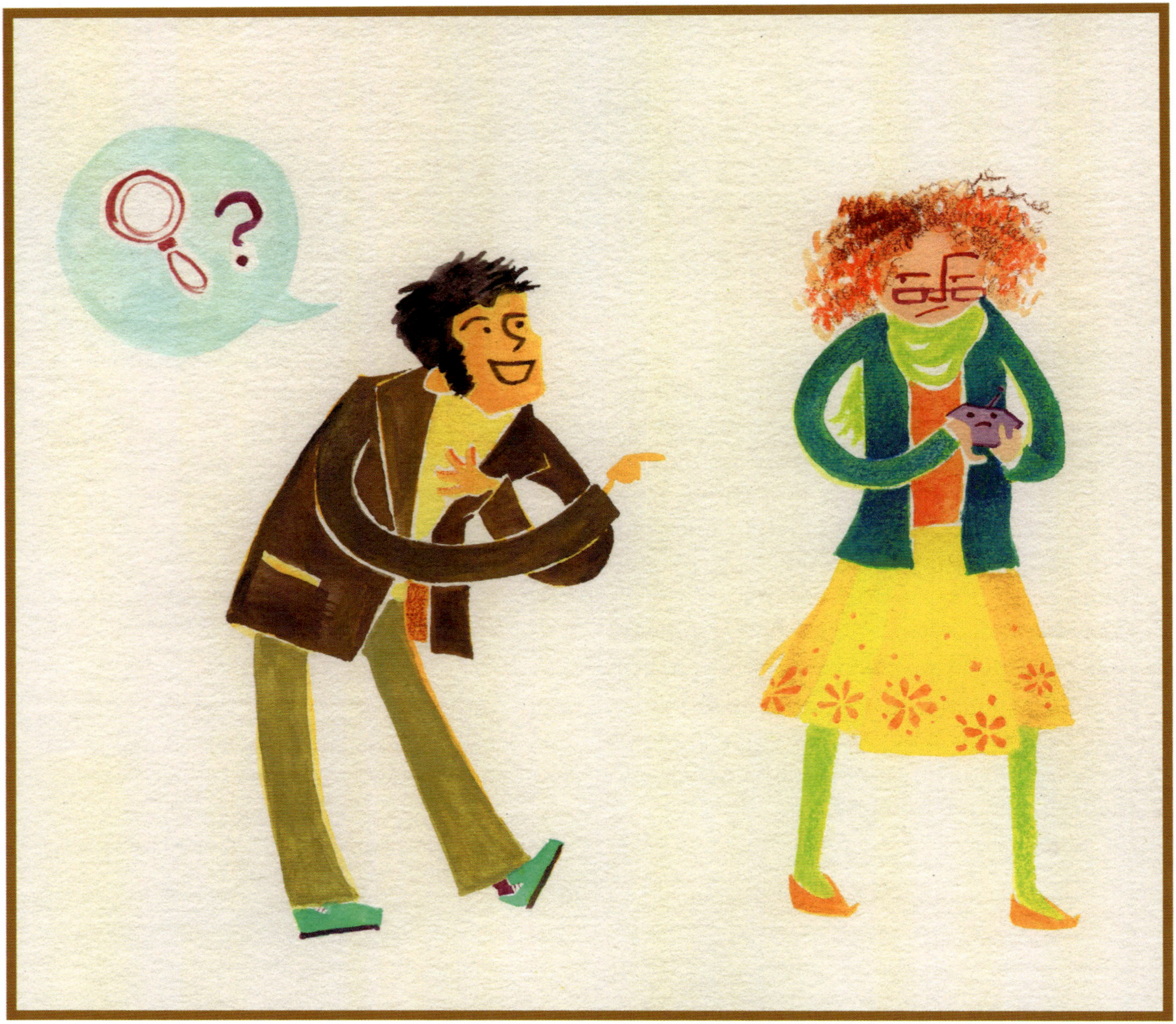

Secondhand Cyborg

"Hey, can you Google that for me?"

The term **Secondhand Cyborg** describes a person who uses technology through someone else. Examples include borrowing a cell phone or asking someone to look something up online.

The advent of the personal cell phone makes individuals increasingly reluctant to let strangers borrow their phone. This is due to the increase in personal information and identity stored on individual devices.[1] People used phones in two ways before the cell phone. Landlines were owned by households and stored in specific rooms in ones home. Public telephone booths were accessible by people on the go. Booths provided temporary privacy for individuals who wished to have a private conversation in public. Personal information was stored in black books, address books or in one's brain. The advent of the mobile phone shifted the storage of connections from external books and one's brain into the phone itself, making the device a much more valuable and personal object.

References

1. Karlson, Amy K. Brush, Bernheim A.J., Schechter, Stuart. (April 2009) Can I Borrow Your Phone? Understanding Concerns When Sharing Mobile Phones. *Microsoft Research. Proceedings of CHI 2009. Association for Computing Machinery, Inc.* Retrieved March 2013, from http://research.microsoft.com/pubs/77555/PhoneSharingCHI2009.pdf

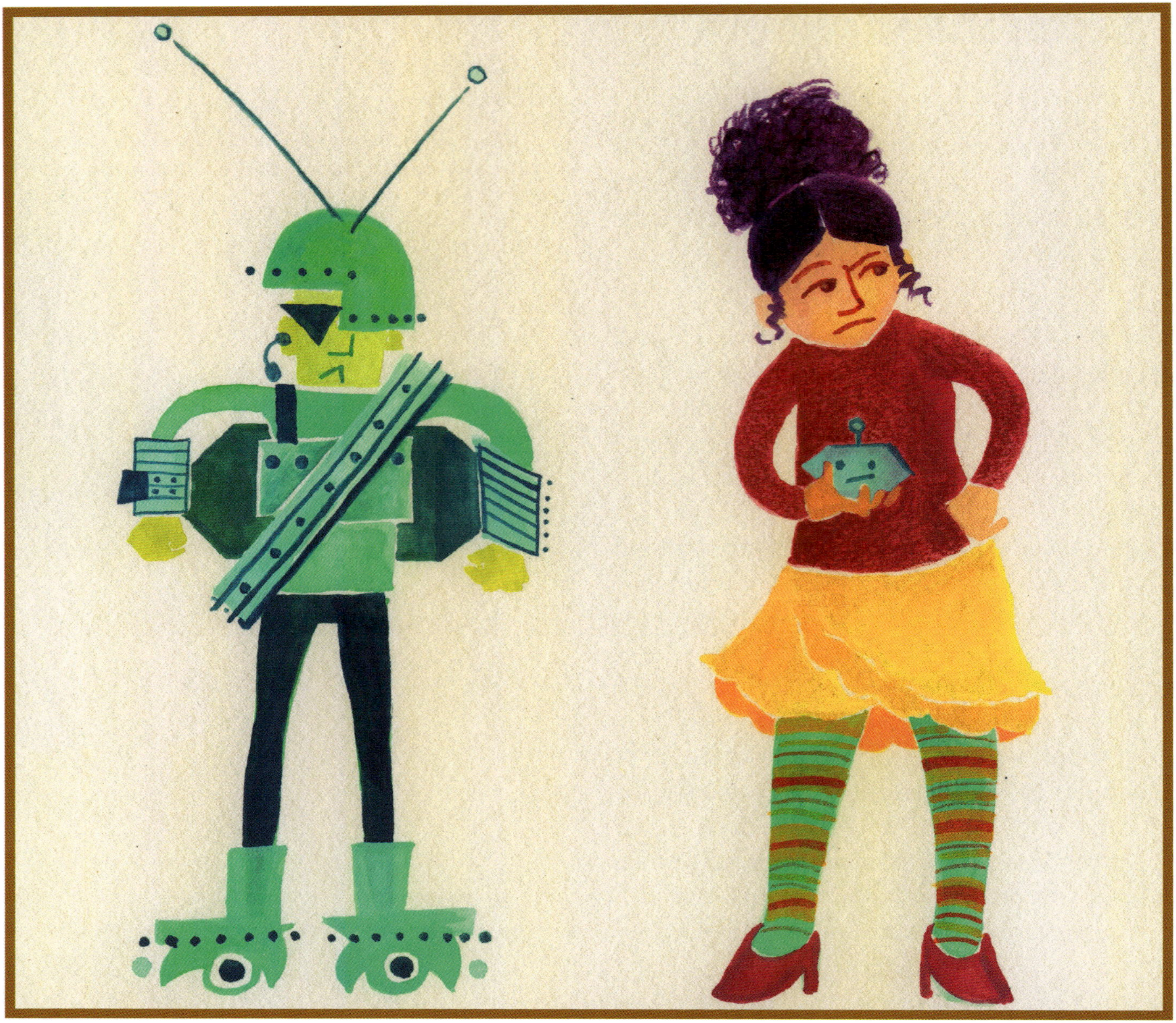

Sighborg

The term **Sighborg** is used to define a person who has become a low-tech cyborg through gradual adaptation and acquisition of technical capabilities and external prosthetics.[1] After noticing this, the user is locked into a never-ending series of upgrades, purchase cycles, and subscription plans. When looking at all of this objectively, especially over a period of time that begins with the user completely uninvolved with technology, the user, looking back on their historical freedom from technology, looks at the phone in their hand or the computer at their desk, and sighs.

References

1. Hess, David. (1995) On Low-tech Cyborgs. In C. H. Gray, H. Figueroa-Sarriera, S. Mentor (Eds.) *The Cyborg Handbook* (pp. 371-78). New York: Routledge.

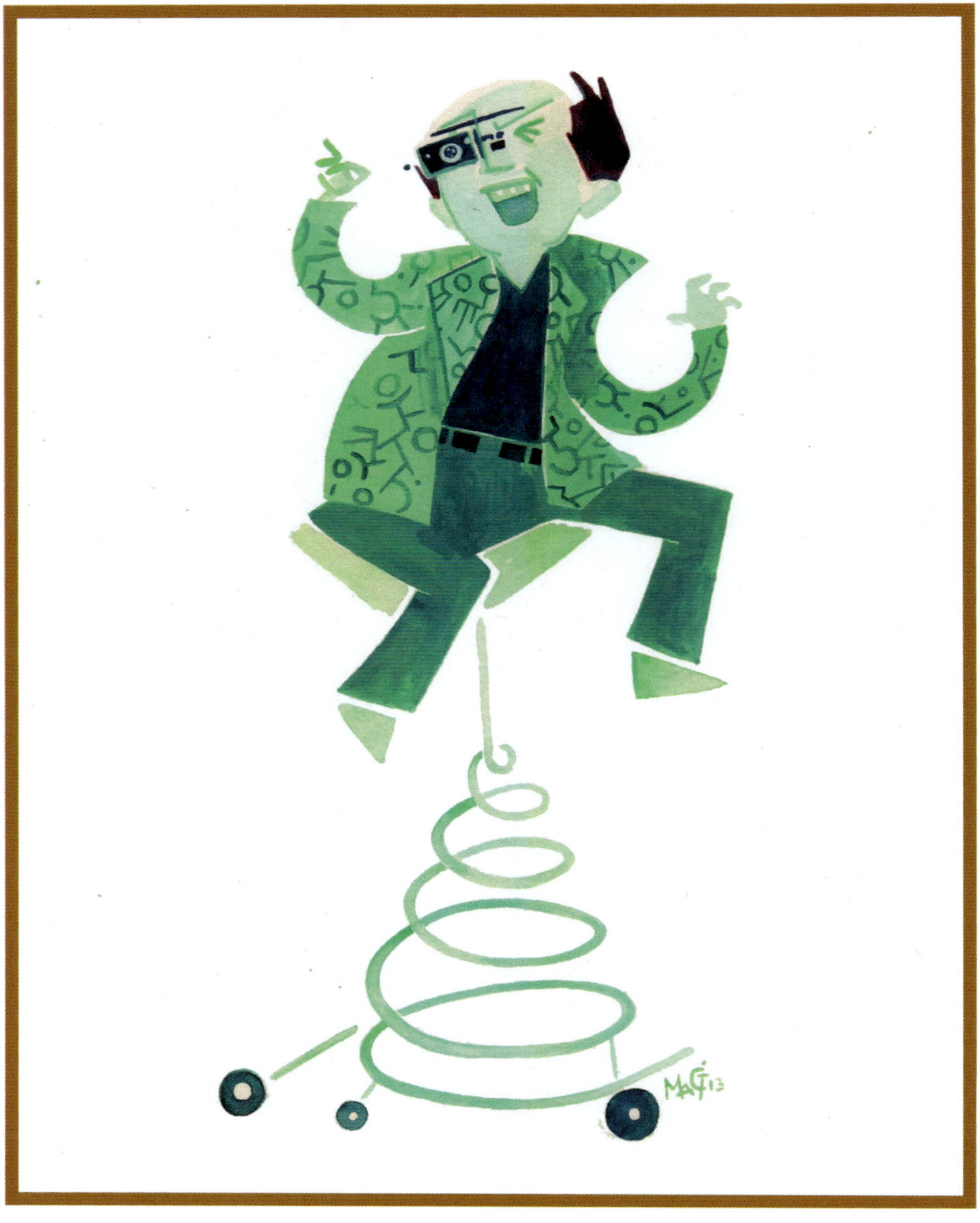

Steve Mann

Dr. Steve Mann, born 1962, in Ontario, Canada, is a living laboratory for the cyborg lifestyle. He is one of the more prominent members of the wearable computing community. Of his many collaborators, James Fung, Chris Aimone, and neurologist Ariel Garten have worked most closely with him on machine vision for wearable heads up displays and the hydraulophone. He is known more recently for being physically removed from a McDonald's restaurant in France for wearing a wearable camera attached to a heads up display.[1]

Dr. Mann believes computers should be designed to organically fit human needs rather than requiring humans to adapt to traditionally stationary technology.

Mann first experimented with wearable computing in high school in the 70s.[2] At MIT he bristled with electronics, wearing many pounds of computing equipment to class. In 1994 Mann introduced the "Wearable Wireless Webcam," a mechanism that streamed images to a webpage in near real time[3] allowing others to comment on Mann's whereabouts. Moore's Law continuously reduced the form factor of Mann's devices; equipment that was heavy 30 years ago is now virtually invisible on the frames of his glasses.

Dr. Steve Mann authored more than 200 publications, including his 2001 book, *Cyborg: Digital Destiny and Human Possibility in the Age of the Wearable Computer* which provides a popular culture view of day-to-day cyborg life. *CYBERMAN*, a feature film about his life and work, was released the same year.[4] Mann's work touches a wide range of disciplines from implant technology to sousveillance (inverse surveillance), privacy, cyber security and cyborg law. Mann received a PhD in Media Arts and Sciences from MIT in 1997.[5] His research and activities can be found online at wearcam.org and eyetap.org.

References

1. Mann, Steve. (2012) Physical assault by McDonald's for wearing Digital Eye Glass. *EyeTap Personal Imaging Lab*. Retrieved January 2013, from http://eyetap.blogspot.com/2012/07/physical-assault-by-mcdonalds-for.html

2. Rhodes, Bradley. (2001) A brief history of wearable computing. *MIT Wearable Computing*. Retrieved January 2013, from http://www.media.mit.edu/wearables/lizzy/timeline.html#1981b

3. Mann, Steve. (1997) An historical account of the 'WearComp' and 'WearCam' inventions developed for applications in Personal Imaging. In The First International Symposium on Wearable Computers: Digest of Papers. (pp. 66–73). IEEE Computer Society.

4. Cyberman. *IMDB*. Retrieved January 2013, from http://www.imdb.com/title/tt0301145/

5. Mann, Steve. *MIT Alumni*. Retrieved January 2013, from http://alumni.media.mit.edu/~steve/

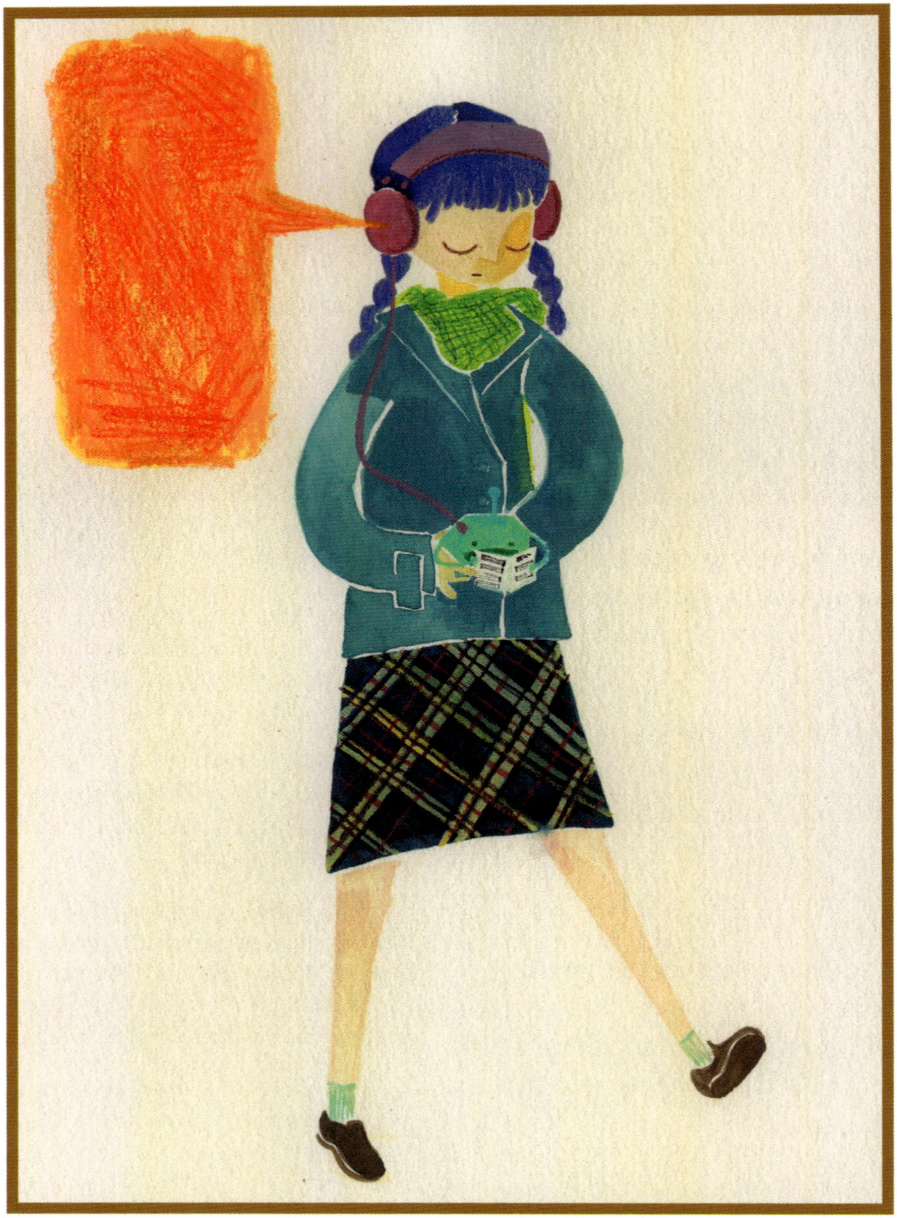

Synesthesia

Synesthesia describes a "condition in which one type of stimulation evokes the sensation of another."[1] Synesthesia is a relatively uncommon in humans, affecting an average of one in 2000 individuals.[2] There are many different kinds of synesthesia. Color-grapheme synesthesia describes the phenomenon of associating and seeing specific colors when thinking of or seeing letters and numbers. Not all color preferences line up. "Most color-grapheme synesthetes perceive the alphabet in their own color scheme, with each letter possessing a different hue."[3]

Other synesthetes report literally seeing sound or hearing color. Richard Cytowic, author of *The Man Who Tasted Shapes*, describes meeting a man who, while eating, saw points in front of his eyes associated with taste.[4]

Cyborg Synesthesia

There are an increasing number of cases of technological-induced synesthesia. Some notable examples include Daniel Kish's work as a blind psychologist who uses echolocation to "see" by clicking his tongue.

Neil Harbisson has the rare condition of achromatopsia, a hereditary vision disorder that only allows him to perceive black and white.

When Harbisson told cyberneticist Adam Montandon of his condition, Montanton built an assemblage for the colorblind artist. The device allowed Harbisson to hear colors, even those beyond the range of human sight. The Eyeborg device had the unique capability to record color and convert it into sound for Harbisson. This allowed him to "hear a symphony of color" as well as "listen" to faces and paintings. As of 2012, Harbisson's Eyeborg device allowed him to perceive 360 different hues, one for each degree on the color wheel.[5] Harbisson demonstrated this synesthetic device, called the "Eyeborg" in a TED talk in July 2012.[6] He anticipates bringing even more capabilities to the device as well as making devices for others with monochromatism, the inability to see color.

In Fall 2004, German systems administrator Udo Wächter began wearing a directional sensing belt dubbed the "Feelspace belt" as part of a research project to investigate the effects of long-term stimulation with orientation information on humans led by Prof. Dr. Peter König at the University of

Synesthesia (cont'd)

Osnabrück.[7] The Feelspace belt was lined with 13 piezoelectric pads than encircled his waist when worn. This belt allowed him to feel a sense of direction no matter which direction he faced. The piezoelectric motor that was facing north at any given moment would constantly buzz, letting Wächter always know which direction he was facing. Osnabrück wore the belt for six weeks straight starting in the Fall of 2004. Wächter's sixth sense of direction even carried itself into his dreams.[8]

Today, a company called Sensebridge sells a DIY Feelspace, or "haptic compass" kit called the North Paw. The company operates out of Noisebridge, a hackerspace in San Francisco, California, and hacklab.to, a hackerspace in Toronto, Canada.[9]

References

1. Synesthesia. *Dictionary.com Unabridged.* Retrieved August, 2013, from http://dictionary.reference.com/browse/Synesthesia

2. Baron-Cohen S, Burt L, Smith-Laittan F, Harrison J, Bolton P. (1996) Synaesthesia: prevalence and familiarity. In *Perception.* (pp. 1996;25(9):1073-9) Cambridge: Department of Environmental Psychology, University of Cambridge.

3. Witthoft, Nathan and Jonathan Winawer. (2012) Learning, Memory, and Synesthesia. In *Psychological Science.*

4. Cytowic. Richard E. (August 2003) *The Man who Tasted Shapes.* Cambridge: MIT Press.

5. Montandon, Adam. Colourblind Eyeborg Colours to Sound. Retrieved February 2013, from http://www.adammontandon.com/neil-harbisson-the-cyborg/

6. Harbisson, Neil. (June 2012) I listen to color. *TEDGlobal.* Retrieved February 2, 2013, from http://www.ted.com/talks/neil_harbisson_i_listen_to_color.html

7. feelSpace: Report of a Study Project. (May 2005) *Universität Osnabrück. Institute of Cognitive Science Department of Neurobiopsychology.* Retrieved April 22, 2011, from http://cogsci.uni-osnabrueck.de/~feelspace/downloads/feelSpace_finalReport.pdf

8. Bains, Sunny. (March 2007) Mixed Feelings. *Wired Magazine.* Retrieved April 22, 2011, from http://www.wired.com/wired/archive/15.04/esp.html

9. North Paw. Retrieved April 2011, from http://sensebridge.net/projects/northpaw/

93

Additional Reading

Ito, Mizuko. (2003) *A New Set of Social Rules for a Newly Wireless Society.*

Helmreich, Stefan. (2008) *After Culture - Reflections on the Apparition of Anthropology in Artificial Life, a Science of Simulation.*

Berman, Marshall. (1982) *All That is Solid Melts into Air: The Experience of Modernity.*

Goffman, Erving. (1963) *Behavior in Public Places; Notes on the Social Organization of Gatherings.*

Haraway, Donna; Hankamer, Jorge; Lease, Gary (1999) *Between Nature & Culture Cyborgs, Simians, Dogs, Genes & Us.*

Leonard, Andrew. (1997) *Bots: The Origin of New Species.*

Boellstorff, Tom. (2010) *Coming of Age in Second Life*

Poster, Mark (2004) *Consumption and Digital Commodities In the Everyday.*

Moore, Gordon E. (1965) *Cramming More Components Onto Integrated Circuits by Gordon.*

Benedikt, Michael. (1991) *Cyberspace: First Steps.*

Downey, Gary Lee; Dumit, Joseph; Williams, Sarah (1995) *Cyborg Anthropology.*

Kellner, Douglas and Best, Stephen. (1983) *Deluze and Guattari, Schizos, Nomas, Rhizomes.*

Anderson, M. T. (2002) *Feed.*

Bernard, Russ. (2000) *Handbook of Methods of Cultural Anthropology.*

Haraway, Donna. (2003) *The Haraway Reader.*

Oulasvirta, Antti; Tamminen, Sakari, Roto, Virpi; Kuorelahti, Jaana (2005) *Interaction in 4-Second Bursts: The Fragmented Nature of Attentional Resources in Mobile HCI.*

Goffman, Erving. (1982) *Interaction Ritual: Essays on Face-to-Face Behavior.*

Johnson, Steven A. (1999) *Interface Culture.*

Bauman, Zygmunt. (2000) *Liquid Modernity.*

Varnelis, Kazys. (2012) *Networked Publics.*

Augé, Marc. (1995) *Non-Places: Introduction to an Anthropology of Supermodernity.*

Additional Reading cont'd

Plant, Sadie. (2004) *On the Mobile; the Effects of Mobile Telephones on Social and Individual Life.*

Lakoff, George. (1999) *Philosophy in the Flesh.*

Latour, Bruno. (2007) *Reassembling the Social: An Introduction to Actor-Network-Theory.*

Durkheim, Emile. (1997) *Suicide, a Study in Sociology.*

Horst, Heather and Miller, Daniel. (2006) *The Cell Phone: An Anthropology of Communication*

Gray, Chris Hables. (1995) *The Cyborg Handbook.*

Biocca, Frank. (1997) The Cyborg's Dilemma - Progressive Embodiment in Virtual Environments.

Turner, Victor. (1967) *The Forest of Symbols.*

de Certeau, Michael; Giard, Luce; Mayol, Pierre (1988) *The Practice of Everyday Life.*

Smith, Marquard and Morra, Joanna (Eds.) (2005) *The Prosthetic Impulse: From a Posthuman Present to a Biocultural Future.*

Schivelbusch, Wolfgang. (1986) *The Railway Journey: The Industrialization of Time and Space in the 19th Century.*

De Kerckhove, Derrick. (1998) *The Skin of Culture: Investigating the New Electronic Reality.*

Weiser, Mark. (1993) *Ubiquitous Computing.*

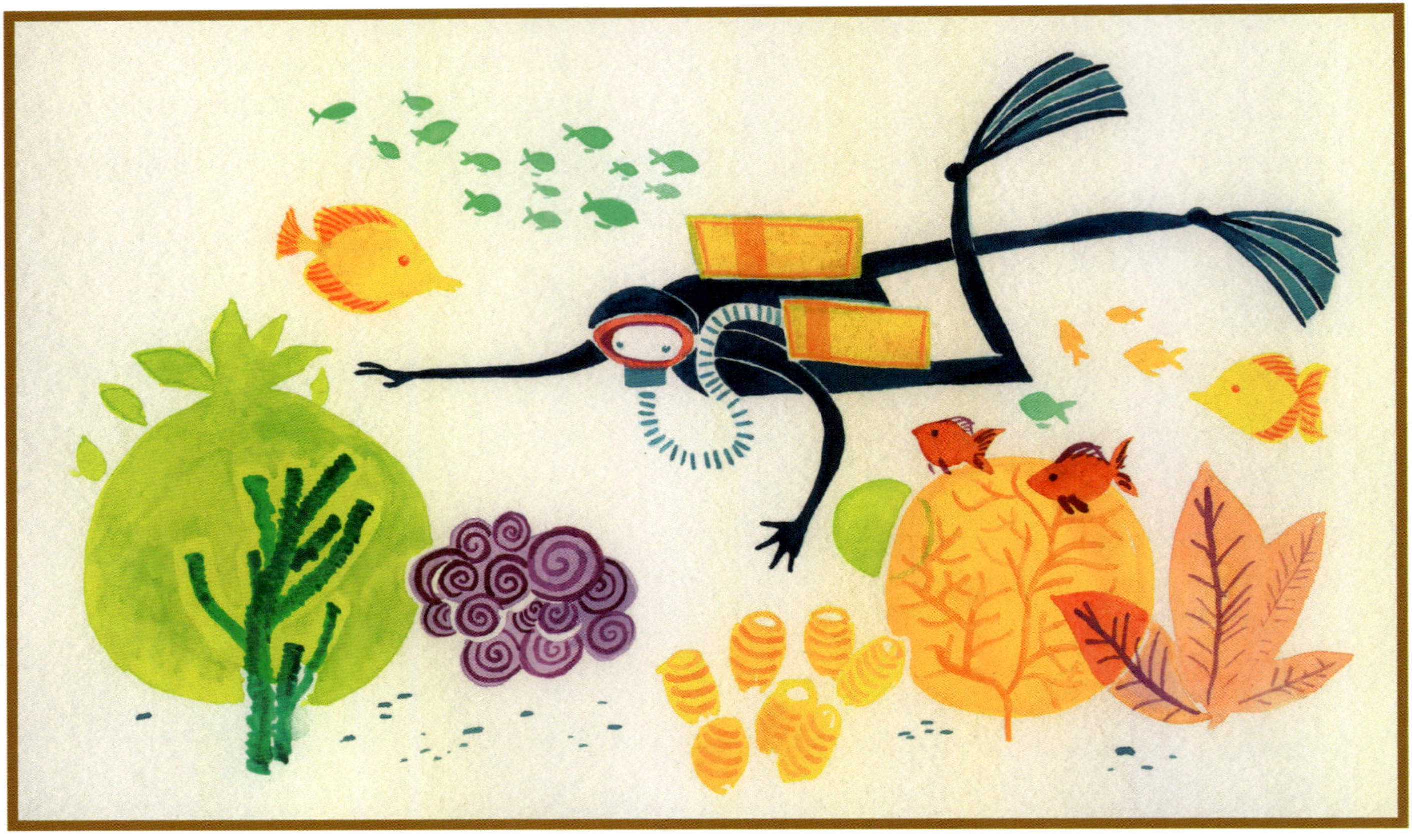

cyborganthropology.com

A Digital Resource

CyborgAnthropology.com is meant to connect many different people across multiple disciplines as well as those involved in the field of Cyborg Anthropology itself. The site is a collection of journals, conferences, papers, books, and curriculum that can be used by anyone.

In the same way that the Internet grows and changes, the field of Cyborg Anthropology must be a flexible field capable of absorbing, classifying and understanding new phenomena, cultural change, and the digital world. To reflect this, cyborganthropology.com is a Wiki. CyborgAnthropology.com runs on MediaWiki, the same software that Wikipedia.org runs on. Aaron Parecki created a visual theme for the site, as well as a number of custom plugins. Anyone is free to edit and add to the site.

Site Submissions

CyborgAnthropology.com welcomes contributions in the form of book reviews, conference listings, journal articles, journal lists, films and film reviews, glossary terms, tools and pieces of critical analysis. If you'd like to contribute any of these items, or have ideas on what to contribute, please go to cyborganthropology.com/contributing

About the Author

Amber Case has been exploring and speaking about the field of Cyborg Anthropology since 2005. Since then, she has been featured in Forbes, WIRED, and many other publications, both in the United States and around the world.

Case grew up knowing that technology would play an increasingly important role in everyday life, and was always looking for new ways of understanding its relationship with people. When Case stumbled upon the newly formed field of Cyborg Anthropology in college, she knew she had to learn more. This book is a brief glimpse into some of the subjects related to the field. There is far more to explore and discover.

In 2010, Case founded Geoloqi, Inc., a software company that made location-based mobile software for developers and businessess. Geoloqi was acquired by GIS software maker Esri in 2012. She was named a National Geographic Emerging Explorer in 2012.

You can read more about the author at http://caseorganic.com

Photo Credit: Aaron Parecki (aaronparecki.com)

About the Illustrator

Maggie Wauklyn has been interested in art ever since she could hold a crayon. She drew in all the margins of her spelling worksheets. On several occasions she received permission to use the big stapler in the office to reassemble the classroom's drawing books' disintegrating pages. During the summer she would take over the family garage and turn it into a painting studio.

After attending college at a state school she moved to Portland, Oregon to focus on her own work. Deftly sitting astride the line between representation and abstraction, her work focuses on the emotional essence of the subject rather than a realistic depiction. To her, illustration is best suited for those things that cannot be photographed, things our wonderful minds experience: imagination, feeling, and wonder.

You can read about the illustrator at http://simplykumquat.com

Notes

Notes

Notes

Notes

Notes

Printed in Great Britain
by Amazon